How to
Locate Jobs
and Land Interviews

Second Edition

How to Locate Jobs and Land Interviews

Second Edition

by Albert L. French

Career Press
180 Fifth Ave.
P.O. Box 34
Hawthorne, NJ   07507
1-800-CAREER-1
201-427-0229 (outside U.S.)
FAX: 201-427-2037

How to Locate Jobs and Land Interviews
(Second Edition)
ISBN 1-56414-059-8, $10.95
Cover design by Harvey Kraft
Printed by Bookmart Press

To order this title by mail, please include price as noted above, $2.50 handling per order, and $1.00 for each book ordered. Send to: Career Press, Inc., 180 Fifth Ave., P.O. Box 34, Hawthorne, NJ 07507

Or call Toll-free 1-800-CAREER-1 (Canada: 201-427-0229) to order using VISA or MasterCard, or for further information on books from Career Press.

Attention: Schools, Organizations, Corporations

This book is available at quantity discounts for bulk purchases for educational, business or sales promotional use.

Please contact: Career Press
180 Fifth Avenue, Box 34
Hawthorne, NJ 07507
or call 1-800-CAREER-1

DEDICATION

This book is lovingly dedicated to my mother and late father, Dorothy and Leo French. They taught me patience, understanding and a respect for work of every kind. They opened my eyes to the exciting and wonderful world around me. They taught me to see beauty in the simple and simplicity in the complex. They encouraged me to question and to become involved. They taught me to love and to give.

Perhaps the old Chinese Proverb, often quoted around our home, best sums up what they gave me.

> *Give a man a fish, and you feed him for a day.*
> *Teach a man to fish, and you feed him for a lifetime.*

This edition is also dedicated to my wife, Jennifer. She has served as my editor, project *ramrod* and Best Friend. She always provided a gentle hand and unswerving dedication. Her constant love, support, input and encouragement are the basic ingredients that fueled this project.

In the final analysis this book, and all the possibilities it holds, is dedicated to you, the reader.

ACKNOWLEDGEMENTS

I wish to express particular thanks to my editor, Betsy Sheldon, for her assistance and patience in the final development of this project.

Special thanks also go to Harry Pash, a fellow writer and merciless proofreader. I guarantee any errors you find must fall to the typesetter.

I also owe a debt of gratitude to Walter Gibson, Program Development, Colorado Department of Labor & Employment; Robert McIntosh, District Sales Manager, Contacts Influential; and Sharon Hallett, Adv. and Promotions Manager, American Directory Publishing Co., Inc. They were always available and responsive to my questions and requests for information and data.

Many thanks to the Denver media for their interest, comments and support in helping to make their audiences aware of this book. My hat is off especially to *The Denver Post;* Keith Wineman, KOA-Radio 85; Alan Dumas, KNUS-Talk Radio; Channel 4 News; Channel 9's Sylvia Jennings, "Good Afternoon Colorado"; Stormy Rottman, Channel 6 *Senior Showcase* and many more for helping me help others.

Also hats off to Joan Pearce, Kurt Van, Jana Patrei, Rayna Lipstein, Nadine Pollard and Marlene Hilkemeier. Their input and experience as professional placement counselors in a 34-year-old company have added a new dimension to the value of quality, professional, employment agencies.

Thanks go out to the national print and electronic media for your assistance in introducing this book across the country. Without this exposure, we might have never met.

A special debt of gratitude goes to the cities of New Orleans, Louisville, Pittsburgh, Detroit, Houston and Tampa who invited me to present training seminars in their communities. These seminars have allowed me to meet and talk with thousands of you personally. Your questions, input and suggestions have played a major role in this new edition. Again, thank you for the assist.

Also to Senior's Inc., United Way and Arapahoe Community College, to mention but a few of the many groups and organizations that have played a role in the development of this book... many thanks.

Space limitations and approaching old age do not allow me to mention by name all those who have played a significant role in the writing and preparation of this book. To all those who are not specifically mentioned, please know my gratitude and appreciation.

Table of Contents

• Section 5   41

- • "THE EMPLOYMENT INTERVIEW ...Setting the Hook
  - • Key traits employers always look for
  - • Anatomy of an employment interview
  - • Typical interview questions
  - • Suggested answers for the tough questions
  - • Interview protocol:
  - *...Guidelines for a successful employment interview*

• Appendices

WHEN A HARVEST IS ASSURED
DON'T EAT THE SEED

You can do, be or have almost anything you desire if you apply the seven steps I will detail on the following pages. Although the focus here is on locating and landing the job you really want, the same principals or steps can be applied to almost any goal you set – losing weight, getting a college degree, becoming financially independent, etc. So these steps will be easy to remember – I'll use the acronym SUCCEED.

The first law of nature that you must recognize is that there is one element we all share in common. No matter how rich, how well educated, how old, we all have 24 hours in a day...that's 86,400 seconds. As each second ticks off, it is gone forever....never to be reclaimed. No one has any more or any less of this precious element than you. The playing field is level. The key is *how you use your time.* "If you do what you've always done, you'll get what you've always gotten." Three years from now each of us will be three years older. Where you are, what you have, and how you will be living is determined only by how you use your time. Each of us, three years from now, will have spent the same amount of time. Each of us will be at different accomplishment levels. The primary difference will be... *how we have spent that time.*

Once you realize time as a common unchanging law and that you and you alone are in control of how you use that time, you have made the first giant step in your great adventure. You are ready to set sail toward almost any port you desire.

Since your purpose in picking up this book is to locate and land the job you need and/or truly want, that will be the focus.

S • Set your goal. See it clearly.

U • Understand the elements or steps necessary to reach that goal.

C • Commit 100 percent of your time and effort required to accomplish each element.

C • Confidence. Never look back once you have made that commitment. Lack of confidence will be your greatest enemy.

E • Experience: If schooling or additional training is required, get it. You have the same amount of time as anyone else.

E • Enthusiasm: A positive mental attitude generates momentum.

D • Determination combined with tenacity *will* produce the goals you set.

Unemployment...

"A man willing to work, and unable to find work, is perhaps the saddest sight that fortune's inequality exhibits under this sun."

...*Thomas Carlyle*

Method...

"There is always a best way to do everything, even if it be to boil an egg."

... *Emerson*

Choice...

"He who chooses the beginning of a road chooses the place it leads to. It is the means that determine the end."

...*Harry Emerson Fosdick*

INTRODUCTION

Although almost every adult becomes a job hunter one or more times during his/her career, we have had little training in how to go about it. As a former teacher, I am acutely aware of this void in both high school and college curriculum.

With the hindsight of a grandfather who spent 11 years in the classroom, 14 in educational publishing, and 8 as an employer in my own business, I felt it was about time that this subject was addressed.

Rather than compile a philosophical treatise on the subject, I've chosen to cut through a lot of verbiage and provide you with a nuts-and-bolts guide to the job hunt in your own specific community.

The Mission of This Book

- To provide the reader with a *proactive*, rather than *reactive* method for locating the vast reservoir of locally available jobs, plus a proven method of generating job interviews. This process or method is used by professional search and placement firms.

- To provide the reader with the local sources and resources for locating virtually every *local firm in your community* by type of business (S.I.C.), including the address, zip, phone and in many cases the key contact person within that business.

- To examine in detail the necessary job-hunt tools; the resume, cover letter and thank-you note.

Many economists consider a 5-percent unemployment rate as *"full employment."* Just consider the number of unemployed people that figure includes. My telephone book lists approximately 400 residences per page. Assuming only one person per residence, that means that on each page there are approximately 20 who are unemployed; even when the economy is considered at *"full employment."*

But that is only the tip of the iceberg. These governmental statistics do not include:

- Those who are still without a job after their unemployment insurance has run out.

- Those just entering the job force as a new graduate, displaced homemaker, retiree, etc.

- The vast number who are "under-employed."

- Those of you who wish to change careers to something that would provide better income opportunities, be more satisfying or make better use of your training, skills and/or experience.

- Those of you who are experienced workers forced into early retirement. Then there are also growing numbers of seniors, "older workers," who wish to get back into the harness because of need or desire.

- Those of you who are "stuck" in a job with little or no chance of growth and must mark time until retirement.

- Those of you forced to accept a miserable working environment, poor benefits or long daily commutes, etc.

- Those of you caught in a paycheck-to-paycheck existence.

Look at that telephone page again and guess how many more are there who are not included in the statistics. To that add those who cannot start the week by exclaiming, *"Thank God it's Monday!"* If you fall into any of these categories, read on...

No matter what your situation, this book is dedicated to teaching you how to locate the job you want and/or need in the location you desire; and how to land an interview with the decision-maker.

You will find the directories listed in Appendix 4 direct you to resources available in virtually every community in every state.

Whether you wish to stay in your present location or move across the country, I've provided you with specific resources for your job search.

Your job hunt can be either a frustrating, frightening experience or an exciting adventure where you can stalk and *bag the trophy* you have always wanted. The choice is yours. It all depends on your *attitude* and your *plan*. If your financial need is critical, you may need to have a two-step plan. Here you take the first available job that meets your immediate need. By doing this you also provide yourself the time necessary to continue your "trophy" hunt (see *Income Goal Worksheet* at the end of the Introduction).

Speaking of time...how long will it take? At best, this is difficult to predict. It depends on a number of factors. If you are willing to accept any job it will obviously take less time than going after the "trophy." Other factors include your job goals, credentials and the amount of time and effort you have and/or are willing to commit. If you are unemployed and experiencing financial pressures, you can and should commit 100 percent of your time to the task. *Getting the job is your full-time job* (see *Job Search Time Guide Worksheet* at the end of the Introduction).

If you're not under pressure and your job hunt is a "moonlighting" project, then of course you will probably commit less time to the effort. *As a rule of thumb, as a full-timer you can expect to spend a week for each $2,000 income you are seeking.* For example, if your goal is a job with an annual income of $10,000, you can expect to spend 5 weeks. If your goal is $30,000, your search will typically take 15 weeks, etc.

Earlier I spoke of the need for a *proactive* rather than a *reactive* method for job hunting. A reactive job hunter sees or hears of an opening and reacts to it. Typically the untrained job hunter will turn to the "Help Wanted" classifieds as a primary source, but this is a mistake. You see, only about 20 percent of the available jobs in any community are ever advertised. Although the "Help Wanted" classifieds should never be overlooked, they represent only a small sampling of the available jobs. Further, you will find most advertised jobs are entry level, seasonal or high turnover positions. Why? Here are just a few reasons they don't advertise:

- A typical ad will pull between 100 to 300 resumes. The review and screening process is very costly and time-consuming so many employers opt to pay a private placement office to do it for them. Employers would love to hear from you directly and save both the time and money.

- Many employers are putting up with employees they would like to replace, if only they knew *you* were available.

- New jobs appear every day as employees leave their jobs for a variety of personal reasons, such as family commitments, discontent, health, retirement, etc.

Realizing this, you as a *proactive* job hunter will seize the opportunity to go after this treasure trove of job openings knowing that there are firms just waiting and praying for you to call. They are ready to hire you at the drop of a hat if only they knew where to find you. This is where you have the advantage. You will learn how to locate them and how to do your own employer screening prior to introducing yourself.

...So if you are ready, let's roll up our sleeves and go to work!... *Let's first learn to understand and deal with the emotional impact of job loss.*

...Remember...
The *most powerful sentence* in the
English language is composed of
only 10 words and 20 letters.....

If it is to be....
...It is up to me!

JOB SEARCH TIME – A GUIDE

If you are launching a full-time job search, this form may be used to get a rough idea of the time required to secure the job you wish. Figure one week for each $2,000. For example if you are looking for $20,000, your base weeks would be 10. Now modify this number by considering each of the following elements.

Your Present or Last Annual Salary (with bonus) — — — —	$
Your Base of Weeks *(one week for every $2,000 in salary you were receiving.)*	
Competitive Qualifications:	
High – Deduct 20% — — — — — — — — — — — —	
Low – Add 50% — — — — — — — — — — — —	
Not Willing to Take a Risk:	
Multiply by 2 — — — — — — — — — — —	
Personal Characteristics: *(Appearance, Personality, Communication Skills)*	
Excellent – Deduct 20% — — — — — — — — —	
Poor – Add 50% — — — — — — — — — — —	
Requirements: *(Location, benefits, size of company etc.)*	
Critical – Add 20% — — — — — — — — — —	
Not Critical – Deduct 20% — — — — — — — —	
Salary Demands: (if unemployed)	
Increase of 20% or more – add 50% — — — — — — —	
Decrease of 10% or more – Deduct 20% — — — — —	
Salary Demands: (if employed)	
Increase of 20% or more – Add 25% — — — — — —	
Decrease of 25% or more – Deduct 25% — — — — —	
Final Job Search Time in Weeks: — — — — — — — — —	

NOTE:
If your Final Job Search Time in Weeks is lower than your base number at the top, use the original number.

- Don't attempt to use this guide if you intend to change careers. Depending on the circumstances, career changes may require additional training, acquiring new skill levels, etc.

- Don't attempt to use this guide if you are not launching a Full-Time Job Search.

INCOME - GOAL WORKSHEET

MONTHLY INCOME		MONTHLY EXPENSES	WANT	NEED
Salary - Self				
Other - Family Income		Rent - Share		
		Rent - All		
		Mortgage		
Child Support		Utilities		
Alimony		Phone		
Other i.e. Investments, Rentals, etc.		Transportation		
		Food		
		Clothing		
		Car Insurance		
Total		Life Insurance		
W-4 # Claimed		Health Insurance		
Checking Acct. Yes ☐ No ☐		Loans - Car		

OTHER ASSETS	Want	Have	Loans - Other		
Savings, IRA etc.					
Other Liquid Assets			Charge Accounts		
			Charge Cards		
Home Equity			Doctor		
Total Assets			Dentist		
COMMENTS:			Lawyer		
			Entertainment		
			Child Care		
			Health Club		
			Cable		
			Other Monthly Exp.		
			Sub Total		
			Less Other Income		
			Net Total $ Required		
			Fed/State Tax @ 25%		
			Sub Total		
			Fee @ $		
			Total Monthly Income		
			Hourly		
			Annual		

The "Big Bang": Who?... Me?

- Understanding Typical Reactions to Job Loss
- Dealing with Stress and Self-Esteem

UNDERSTANDING TYPICAL REACTONS TO JOB LOSS

Change in our lives can, and usually does, create stress that affects us emotionally. A certain amount of stress, such as having to make a decision, meeting a deadline or quota, etc., is good and provides us with energy, motivation and direction.

A *major change or crisis,* however, such as a divorce, the death of a loved one, etc., can become overwhelming and crippling. Job loss, like a death or divorce, is such a crisis change. It can create a tidal wave crippling us socially, emotionally, physically and financially.

Typically, the reduction of income is the first noticeable change in the household. As the period of unemployment lengthens the emotional impact and the resulting stress becomes greater. Together these factors can damage otherwise stable family or personal relationships. Additionally such feelings stand in our way to regaining employment. *Understanding and taking action to control these negative effects becomes our number-one job.*

Although our jobs provide us with money and thereby a particular standard of living, they also make us feel productive and useful...to ourselves, our families and society. Our jobs give us a sense of belonging and contributing to a group...whether it be our work unit, company or our union. Frequently, when we are asked about who we are, we describe ourselves in terms of our work. "I'm a firefighter." "I work for University Hospital as a nurse." Thus our identities and self-respect are dependent on our jobs to a great extent. The sudden loss of employment causes disruptions in our lives, reorders our priorities (both personal and financial) and damages our self-esteem. Many people are not adequately prepared to handle the stress of unemployment. They are unable to deal with the emotional strain upon family relationships, friendships or the anxiety of possibly relocating to a new area.

Like all major changes in our lives, the fear of the *unknown* is a substantial hurdle in coping with unemployment. When we lose our job, we may experience a loss similar to the death of a close friend or relative. And although the degree of emotional loss may be less, most of us will experience a similar grieving process. The Continuum Center of Oakland University has identified the typical stages of grief following job loss. Read through the descriptions below. If you find you are stuck in one stage, you may want to talk to someone, perhaps even a professional counselor about your feelings.

Stage 1. Happiness or shock and denial

Some people at first feel wonderful...happy at having a "vacation" or relief that the waiting is over. For most of us there is a numbness. We don't believe that we really have lost our job, we hope for a recall when that is very unlikely. We don't act, because we do not really accept our loss.

Stage 2. Emotional release

We need to vent our feelings of anger, sadness, frustration, jealousy, etc. Holding in feelings may lead to physical symptoms that may delay moving on to action.

Stage 3. Depression and physical distress

We feel lost and helpless. We doubt our abilities. We may feel hopelessness. We show physical signs of stress such as sleeplessness, loss of appetite or back and stomach problems.

Stage 4. Panic and guilt

We have trouble thinking clearly and cannot plan effectively. We feel responsible for the layoff even though we had no control over it. We keep thinking "if only." We try to do everything at once, and do nothing efficiently.

Stage 5. Anger and hostility

This is an important part of the recovery process. Anger can be positive, but we feel angry at those around us. We need to learn to use these strong feelings to give us the energy to make plans and move on to the next stage. This is the turning point.

Stage 6. Renewed hope and rebuilding

We begin to plan for our new life without the old job. We are able to take constructive action toward obtaining new work.

State 7. Resolution

We let go of our anger and false hopes. We feel in control of our lives again. The loss is still part of us but does not dictate our actions.

DEALING WITH STRESS AND SELF-ESTEEM

Stress is the body's response to demands made upon it. Change is a primary cause of stress. Unemployment forces many changes upon our established routines, spending patterns and aspirations. Not only is our source of income gone, but so is our daily structure, the social interaction of the job and, most importantly, our sense of purpose. And as time goes on, our *self-esteem* and *sense of value* are diminished. But keep in mind that although we may be feeling disorganized or not in control, there are many things we can do to relieve our anxiety and defuse stress.

Communication with others is a key element in reducing stress. Isolation can block our progress to becoming reemployed. Continued social isolation may lead to depression. Any problem is easier to handle if we share it with someone who is concerned. Our problems can be put into perspective when we know people care about us. But they cannot provide help and understanding if they are unaware of our feelings and concerns.

It is not easy to *ask for help* when we are "down" but often this is the time when we need help most. If friends or relatives are unavailable to you, then you should seek out others who are, such as: previous co-workers, clergy or neighbors. If serious problems arise, professional counseling should be considered.

Exercise is an effective way to work off tension. Some form of daily exercise is essential to your physical and emotional well being, whether you choose walking, biking, aerobics or running. Team or group sports like softball or bowling provide both exercise and social interaction. Exercise and healthy competition combined with the attainment of personal physical goals can bolster your bruised self-esteem and enhance your sense of accomplishment. They will leave you renewed and refreshed to face your daily challenges.

Helping others is another means of raising your self-esteem. This can be done in many different ways. Some people use this period of unemployment to establish close relationships with family members. One study suggests that although increased stress is created by job loss, in cases where this stress is handled successfully, there may actually be improved communication between family members. Sometimes you are able to acquire a greater understanding of your family members' abilities and contributions. This may be a time when family activities can be planned and shared together...whether it is a household project or short trip.

Volunteer activities can be rewarding and worthwhile. Occasionally, volunteer work leads to paid employment, although this shouldn't be the primary reason for volunteering. You may be able to upgrade certain job-related skills through volunteer experience.

The key of handling stress and maintaining your self-esteem, however, is to let go of the past and focus on the now; swing into action. The sooner you start, the better.

First plan a budget. As soon as you become aware of a layoff or termination, you should quickly face the financial realities of your job loss. Your income will be lower. By developing budgetary plans early, you can forestall or avoid completely, more severe spending reductions later. Once your spending plans are in place, you will be free to concentrate on your job-search activities. Furthermore, taking these actions may help to reduce anxiety and stress.

Use the *Income–Goal Worksheet* to **Identify where your money is going.** Measure your needs compared to your wants. Prioritize your expenses, giving serious consideration to the basic necessities, mortgage or rent payments, utilities, property taxes, food, health care and transportation expenses. At the first sign of a job loss, reduce or eliminate expenses that you want, but do not need, i.e., entertainment, new clothing, VCR, etc. Above all, do *not take on any new debts* unless absolutely necessary. *Don't forget to budget for your job-hunting expenses.* These will include such items as resume preparation, transportation, postage, employment and/or recruitment fees, etc.

Plan daily accomplishments. When the structure of the work environment is removed, it is all too easy to "fritter" away your time. By planning daily goals into your schedule you are less likely to harm your self-esteem. You should prepare goal lists both daily and weekly. As you complete each task, you should check it off your list. Such routines organize your days and make you aware of your accomplishments. *(**Note:** I have provided helpful Prioritizing Grids for this purpose in Appendix 3.)*

Plan your job search. That is exactly what this book is designed to help you do.

12 TIPS TO OVERCOME THE CRISIS

1. Make no decisions that will cause any more changes until you have had a chance to gain perspective.
2. Talk to people you trust and respect about your situation...this is not the time to go it alone.
3. Talk with your family about your concerns and let them know this affects everyone, and everyone will have to accept responsibilities to help out.
4. Spend time each day looking at the positives in your life...there are always some.

5. Remember not to measure your total self-worth in terms of this situation.

6. Analyze your family spending patterns. If there are things you can do without, cut them from your budget immediately.

7. Write out a budget. *Use your Income – Goal Worksheet.*

8. Contact creditors and explain your situation. Tell them what you are able to pay (even if it is only a few dollars).

9. Start looking immediately for sources of income. Contact your local Job Service Center about filing a claim for unemployment.

10. A Job Service Center counselor may be able to suggest other income sources such as application for food stamps.

11. If you or another member of your family feels unable to cope with the pressures, seek out a counselor for professional help. Counseling may be available through your area Mental Health Center listed in the *yellow pages.*

12. Swing into positive action. Think of the possibilities. If you are busy positively planning and accomplishing tasks each day, you are taking control. The opportunity of starting fresh, meeting new people, learning new skills and finding greater opportunities and rewards can and should be an exciting adventure. By swinging into action you are taking control...you are making things happen. You are using the stress as a motivating tool and an ally.

This book will provide you with the map... the step-by-step process to making those possibilities a reality in your life. Frankly, the loss of your job may just be the opportunity of a lifetime; an opportunity to find everything you have always wanted in a job. Wouldn't it be great to start the week by jumping out of bed and saying... "Thank God it's Monday!" The choice, opportunity and possibilities are yours!

---

* Much of the above is reprinted here from the Colorado Department of Labor & Employment booklet, *Weathering the Crisis; Job Loss 395-80-09-1047 (R2/90)*

How to Locate "The Hidden Job Openings"

. . . . ."Elementary, My Dear Watson. . .Elementary"

- NETWORKING–Casting the Net
- THE PROFESSIONAL'S SECRET REVEALED
  (Business-to-Business Directories)

Preparedness...

"We are all, it seems, saving ourselves for the Senior Prom. But many of us forget that somewhere along the way we must learn to dance."

...Alan Harrington

Opportunity...

"A wise man will make more opportunities than he finds."

...Francis Bacon

Vocations...

"Vocations which we wanted to pursue, but didn't, bleed like colors on the whole of our existence."

...Balzac

NETWORKING – CASTING THE NET

or How You Get Hundreds of Others to HELP in Your Job Search

Networking is a buzzword that we hear a lot, but seldom understand. Basically it is nothing more than asking others to help you locate job openings. Each of the methods listed in the "How People Get Jobs" chart on page 17, is a networking source (applying to the employer, asking friends, using agencies, etc.). Developing and using an Employment Search Network is the key or foundation for the entire job-prospecting process.

The Typical Job Hunter's Approach

Because we've never been taught, most of us tend to be reactive rather than proactive job hunters. That is, we hear of a job or see one advertised and we react by completing an application in the firm's office and/or submitting a resume....along with several hundred other applicants. In the Denver area, for example, an advertised job typically draws 100 to 300 applications. On national television you've seen hundreds of people standing in long lines waiting to apply for a limited number of jobs. If you are a rocket scientist, a Nobel Prize winner, or a 7'8" college basketball star the lines won't be as long...but there will be lines. Believe me, the competition is keen in almost any field.

If you wish to be in the front of the line, you must launch a proactive job search. That is learning and applying the job-search method used by the professional recruiters to locate the vast reservoir of unadvertised jobs. You will find this "hidden market" contains 8 or more of every 10 locally available jobs – plus it offers far less competition. You say, "OK French, that sounds great, but how do I do it and why doesn't everyone?"

11

Answer: Few know about it because they have never been taught – but I'll teach you now.

Not only are few of the available jobs "published" but *most of the good jobs* will *never* make it to the general public. Take another look at the "Help Wanted" ads. You'll find many entry level and high turnover jobs, but few truly good jobs. Most of the good jobs are filled through internal networking. By the time an opening is listed in the firm's personnel office, published in the classifieds, or registered with the state job center etc....major efforts have usually been made to fill the position internally. Secondly, you will note from the chart "How People Get Jobs," that the highest success ratio, double that of any other method, is applying directly to the employer. Since it is the primary source of the so called "hidden job market" and the most effective, in terms of employment success, let's take a careful look at how it works and how to tap its potential.

When I speak of "applying directly to the employer" I'm not suggesting you call the president of of IBM to prospect for a book-keeping position. While the employer in small companies is usually the owner, president or CEO in mid-sized or large companies it may be the CEO, general manager, branch manager, departmental manager, etc. Whatever the title, the person you wish to contact is *the highest local primary decision-maker.* Even if this primary decision-maker is not directly responsible for the hiring decision, you better believe if your call or resume is directed to the appropriate hiring source by the Boss, *it will get special and immediate attention.*

Note: A firm's Personnel or Human Resource Department is NOT the place to prospect for a job. Its function is to evaluate and eliminate job applicants... not to search for them.

Typically the employer is the first to know that Ben, a faithful and valued employee of 20 years, is retiring in six months or that Mary must return to Iowa to care for an ailing parent. The employer is the first to know his company has just won a major contract and must increase the staff. The employer is also aware that he has a very unproductive employee he would love to replace if he could just find the right person.

It is only after the employer is aware of a need that anyone else is alerted. Typically the employer will first ask friends and colleagues for references. Then a notice announcing the opening will be posted on the company bulletin boards. Next the personnel department will become involved; then employment agencies and recruiting offices may be contacted. Finally, when all else has failed, an ad will be placed in the local newspaper.

When job prospecting directly with the employer you are like a "cut off" player in a baseball game. By proactively locating unannounced job openings and acting quickly, you keep the opposing base runners (reactive job hunters) from advancing. And the irony is, they will never know a job opening existed. For example right here, today, job offers have been made and accepted by proactive job applicants. Jobs for which you may be better qualified. The job offer could have been yours if only the employer had known you were available.

Question: How is the employer going to find me?

Answer: Through networking...i.e. prospecting for job openings.

Believe it or not, most people like to help others and are willing to help, if asked. Helping someone makes us feel good. But you must ask, and that can prove very difficult. You see, our job is a part of our personal identity. It can be embarrassing to let others know we have lost our job and are asking for help.

Years ago to be "fired" was a badge of failure. Today the connotation of job loss is changing as the complexion of the job market is changing. It is common today to read of companies down-sizing, laying off, and/or offering early retirement plans. For management level employees, larger companies are turning to "Outplacement" organizations that teach the displaced manager how to locate new jobs. Unfortunately, this training is usually *not* made available to non-management staff.

No matter what word is used to describe your situation, the bottom line is you are out of work and are seeking employment.

Question: "Who do I ask?"
Answer: Everyone!

Family, friends, people you know at work, church, clubs, etc. Each is a networking resource. Another rich resource is people you do business with and the places you shop such as grocery store, insurance agent, tire shop, bank, your tax preparer, barber/salon, lube shop, convenience store, etc. In fact I suggest that you sit down with the index of your telephone yellow pages and look at each heading. This exercise will serve to jog your memory. As you do this you'll be surprised at the number of people you know. Include them in your job search network.

Most of us know at least 200 people. In turn, each of those people knows at least 200 people (200 x 200 x 200, etc.....). Within a week you can have literally hundreds of people helping you in your search. This is the superstructure of networking.

It is obvious, however, from the statistics gathered by the Bureau of Census, that speaking directly with employers is the most productive. Although *I want you to employ every method and resource* in your job search, I'll focus on *how you get employers to network for you.*

Positioned or Power Networking

I call employer contact "positioned or power networking." It is this positioned or power networking that professional recruiters employ when prospecting for the hidden job market. You tap it by approaching the employer directly by telephone. Let's call this "kitchen-table prospecting." There are several reasons for using the phone or "kitchen-table prospecting."

1. Expense: The telephone is inexpensive. In most cases you already have one or you have a friend who has one. It would be costly to travel all over town calling on employers.

2. Attention: A telephone places you at the front of the line. It carries a sense of urgency. When an employer picks up the phone, you get immediate focused attention. This is proven daily by the millions of dollars in sales generated through telemarketing. Mail is pitched or placed in a stack to go through later. This is also the case with your unsolicited resume.

3. Response Time: It takes time to open, read and respond to a letter. How many resumes have you mailed and received no response to? The same information can be gathered by phone in less than a minute. You simply ask a question...and you get an answer.

4. Rapport: By engaging in a telephone conversation with the hiring source, you are developing rapport that cannot be conveyed in a cover letter. In fact, as you speak, you are engaging in a preliminary interview with the hiring source.

5. Efficient: While you are waiting and reading a magazine in the reception room, the employer is busy talking with others on the phone. Let someone else wait while the employer is talking with you. You can make 50 or more telephone calls in less time than you will spend just waiting for the employer to see you. And, if you arrive unannounced, in more cases than you would like to imagine, the person you wish to speak with will not be available. You may be asked to fill out an application or leave your resume. In actuality they are saying,..... "Don't call us. We'll call you."

6. Positioned or Power Networking: And here is most important reason. Out of 100 calls you will typically locate only four or five openings. That means you get 95 "Sorry, but we have no openings." By prospecting for job openings by phone from your kitchen table you can turn each of the 95 "no's" into a potentially powerful networking contact. Here's how it is done. When you get a no, simply ask the follow-up question, "Do you know anyone who might be looking for a _____?" Normally you will receive 10 to 15 referrals from the 95 no's. I call these positioned or power referrals because when you call and use the name of the person who referred you, the employer on the other end of the line puts on his/her "big ears." You get *special attention*. They will feel complimented that you have been given their name.

The Power of Referrals

Every salesperson knows the power of referrals. You will make 10 sales from referrals for every one made through "cold calls." Again, if your contact has no appropriate opening, ask if he or she knows of anyone who might. *You are now building a powerful positioned network of high-profile business owners and primary decision-makers who are assisting you in your job search.*

Here's an actual example of how it works. Recently I was asked by a local church group to help a new Russian immigrant it was sponsoring to locate a clerical position in Denver. Though she had a master's degree in English, all her work experience had been in the former Soviet Union.

While making my regular daily job prospecting calls, I concluded each conversation by asking the employer if he/she knew anyone who needed a person who was extremely fluent in both English and Russian.

16

To make a long story short, within 48 hours, by asking questions of people who had no idea who I was, I had referrals that lead me to three potential international employers and the office of a former U.S. senator and presidential hopeful.

HOW PEOPLE GET JOBS

Job Search Method	% who tried it	Success ratio
Applying directly to employer	66%	48:100
Asking friends about jobs where they work	51%	22:100
Answering local newspaper ads	46%	24:100
Asking friends about jobs elsewhere	42%	12:100
Using the state employment service	34%	14:100
Asking relatives about jobs where they work	28%	19:100
Asking relatives about jobs elsewhere	27%	7:100
Using private employment agency	21%	24:100
Taking a civil service examination	15%	13:100
Using the school placement office	13%	12:100
Answering non-local newspaper ads	12%	10:100
Asking a teacher or professor about jobs	10%	12:100
Union hall hiring	6%	22:100
Using local organizations	6%	13:100
Answering ads in a professional journal	5%	7:100
Placing an ad in a local paper	2%	13:100
Going to where employers pick up people	1%	8:100
Other miscellaneous approaches	12%	40:100

Source: Bureau of Census (poll of 10 million job seekers)

Now you understand the process, the simplicity and power of networking. The next question you should ask is, "How do I put it into action?" That's exactly what I'm going to show you next.

HOW TO LOCATE "THE HIDDEN JOB OPENINGS"

As mentioned previously, only about 20 percent of the available jobs are ever advertised. I will show you how to reach the huge unadvertised, "hidden" 80 percent quickly and easily by using the same methods employed by professional job placement services. And, after the initial visit to your library,

...you can do it while enjoying a cup of coffee at your kitchen table.

Whether you are in desperate need of a job, want to change careers, just entering the work force, re-entering the job market, looking for more money, more challenge or whatever your motivation; this information can help you quickly, easily and efficiently locate job openings before they are ever advertised. And best of all, it's available for your use *free of charge.*

I'm talking about business-to-business directories you will find in your local library. Although they will differ in content and organization, they will provide you with detailed information essential to locating and contacting the 8 out of 10 locally available jobs that will never be advertised.

Since it would be impossible to detail each local directory listed in Appendix 4, I've selected *Contacts Influential* for purposes of demonstration and explanation. Although any single local directory referenced may not be arranged as *Contacts Influential*, each contains information and cross-reference sections common to most business directories.

Though *Contacts Influential* is a city directory you will also find state-wide business directories that include every community in each state (see Appendix 4).

The beauty of using business directories in your job search is that they provide you with a wealth of local information you need for your "kitchen-table" job search:

- Name of business/firm
- Name and title of key personnel
- Complete address including zip code
- Telephone number
- Number of employees
- Kind of business *(Standard Industrial Code Number; S.I.C.)*
- Type of location i.e.. *(Sole Office, Home Office, Branch Office)*
- Number of years in business

(See example on next page)

Another excellent reference is the *American State Directories.* Yearly they publish a state-wide business directory that includes *every community in each state* (except New York). The *American State Directories* classify businesses in much the same way as your telephone yellow page directory. *(See Appendix 4 for your state.)*

Some directories will list firms by yellow page category rather than S.I.C. Other organizational changes may include a Business Telephone Index and a Key Individual Section. Each, however, provides essentially the same information on each business. Just refer to the information relating to the organization of that directory.

HOW TO USE THIS JOB SEARCH TREASURE CHEST

For purpose of explanation I've selected the Denver, Colo., edition of the *Contacts Influential* directory. As mentioned previously, each of the business-to-business directories listed for your location in Appendix 4 will contain essentially the same information though organization and content may vary.

The *Contacts Influential* directory is divided into four sections or listings. Although each listing can be a valuable cross-reference in your job hunting, you will probably find the *listing by S.I.C.* to be your primary resource.

LISTING BY S.I.C.

This section provides a listing of all metro firms arranged numerically by Standard Industrial Classification (S.I.C.) codes. This standard governmental classification system is roughly equal to the telephone company's yellow page classifications.

THESE CLASSIFICATIONS INCLUDE:

- Non-Manufacturing
- Manufacturing
- Transportation, Communication, Electric, Gas & Sanitary Services
- Wholesale Trade
- Retail Trade
- Finance, Insurance & Real Estate
- *Services* *
- Public Administration

* Each of these broad classifications is then further classified under the **99 Major Group Numbers**. For example the heading *"Services"* has 14 Major Groups:

- Hotels and other Lodging Places
- Membership Organizations
- Personal Services **
- Private Households
- Automotive Repair Services and Garages
- Miscellaneous Services
- Miscellaneous Repair Services
- Motion Pictures
- Amusement and Recreation Services
- Health Services
- Legal Services
- Educational Services
- Museums, Botanical and Zoological
- Social Services

** Then each of these Major Groups is further broken down. For example the Major Group *"Personal Services"* includes the following types of firms or businesses:

- Laundry, Cleaning and Garment Services
- Photographic Studios Portrait
- Beauty Shops
- Shoe Repair and Hat Cleaning
- Funeral Service and Crematories
- Miscellaneous Personal Services

ALPHA INDEX TO S.I.C. CODES

Let's say you don't know just where to look under the S.I.C. Code classifications. You can quickly locate it in the Alpha Index to S.I.C. Codes.

Recently I wrote a resume for Helen, a beautician. By using this procedure she quickly located more than 300 beauty shops in the metro area. Here's how.

First we went to the *Alpha Index to S.I.C codes* section. Here she found the S.I.C code number she was looking for...7231. Better yet, it included three types of businesses:

7231   Beauticians

7231   Beauty and Barbershops Combined

7231   Beauty Shops

Armed with this four-digit S.I.C. number, she went to the *Firms Classified by S.I.C.* section where she quickly located more than 300 business listings in the metro area. You will note each listing provides the (1) business name; (2) address; (3) key contact person; (4) Title i.e.: owner, manager, etc.; (5) telephone; (6) whether it is locally owned (L), branch office (B), or headquarters (H); (7) the number of employees at that location.

Sample Listing:

Bea's Beauty Salon   422-2051   L=(Locally Owned) A=(1-5 employees)
5610 Zepher St.   Arvada CO   80002
Sealman, Ms. Bea   Owner

FIRMS BY ZIP CODE

Now let's assume you need to locate a job close to home. Not only is it more convenient, but many find it a necessity. Perhaps you don't have a car, or you have young children and wish to remain close to home. In this case you may wish to contact businesses in your immediate area.

The same detailed information, discussed earlier, is provided for each business within each zip code.

ADDITIONAL HELPFUL INFORMATION FOUND IN DIRECTORIES

Firms Alphabetized:

If you have the name of a company, but need an address, key contact person or telephone number, here is where to look. It is also an ideal source for a little research on the company as you will find information about the type of company or location, number of employees, principals, etc.

Business Telephone Index:

Many times a blind ad will provide only a phone number. A cross-reference Business Telephone Directory is where you can locate the name of the firm placing the ad along with the address. Then by referring to the **Firms Alphabetized** section you will find all the information, discussed earlier, on that business. Available in most libraries.

Key Individual Section:

If you are an aggressive "job seeker," in addition to viewing local TV news programs, you will want to read the Business, Career, and/or Lifestyle sections in your local newspaper... daily. Here you will find articles about new businesses, "movers and shakers," etc. Such activities will keep you informed on job opportunities and trends. In many cases you may have only the name of an individual. A directory containing a **Key Individual Section** will provide an alphabetical listing of key personnel in the area showing name, title, firm name and telephone number. If your available directories do not have a key individual listing, call and ask the editor/ writer/broadcaster for the name of the firm with which the mentioned individual is associated. This will quickly provide the needed information. With that information you can turn to **Firms Alphabetized** for all the details discussed earlier.

Market Planning Section:

This section contains a complete inventory of businesses by type of location, size of business and S.I.C code within each zip code area. This can be a handy research tool. Use the list of S.I.C codes to pick the type of businesses you want to contact. Then use the complete count from the Market Planning Section for each S.I.C. code by zip code to find every prospect in your area. Ask your librarian for assistance.

The Tools

- The Resume
- The Cover Letter

Advertising...

"Doing business [locating a job opening landing an interview without advertising and skills] is like winking at a girl in the dark. You know what you are doing but nobody else does."

...Steuart Henderson Britt

WHAT TO DO FIRST

Before you rush off to your local library you will want to be prepared. Once you have a bite, you must be able to set the hook. To do this you should have:

- a current resume
- a cover letter

Each of these items will require careful planning and preparation.

* You will find helpful worksheets in Appendix 3 of this book.

THE RESUME

In today's job market a well-prepared resume is almost a requirement.

Although *you* are in the best position to *sell* yourself: your talents, skills, etc., you may feel immobilized at the thought of writing a "door-opening" resume. There are several good reasons for that.

- *Schools generally do not teach students how to write resumes.*
- *It is difficult to remain objective when writing about yourself and there is a tendency to say too little or too much.*
- *Resume writing is quite different from other forms of written communication and is awkward for many inexperienced writers.*
- *You may not have the office equipment to produce a professional-looking resume even if you write it yourself.*

There are a number of "How To Write A Resume" books on the market; some are excellent, but they don't quell the fear, replace your lack of experience or overcome the office equipment problem.

(See "Selected Bibliography of Resume Books" in Appendix 3.)

A simple answer is to secure a good professional resume service. When your car needs a grease job and oil change, you normally turn to a specialist. You go to a specialist to get your haircut, your taxes prepared or your teeth cleaned. A professional resume service is no different.

Although the cost of a professionally prepared resume and cover letter will normally run $50 to $150, it very likely is the best money you can spend. There are few investments of $100 that will yield $10,000 to $30,000-plus in return. You will spend more than that on oil changes and haircuts in the course of a year.

Besides, the time you would spend writing might be more wisely spent job prospecting. If you are not a typist or don't have a good typewriter, you will need to hire that done anyway.

Assuming you follow this suggestion, how do you go about locating the resume service you are going to *trust with your future?* This choice can be very important. You should do it with the same care you use in selecting a doctor, dentist, attorney or any other professional. First ask your friends and associates for recommendations. Check the ads in the newspaper and yellow pages...Then call and ask questions. As a prospective employer, you have every right to interview them first. You will find some are true professionals while others may be typing and secretarial services that write resumes on the side. After you have qualified available resume services by phone, you will want to make a personal visit before making a final selection. *Remember you are placing your job future in the hands of this writer.* Here are some things you will want to know. Some answers you can get on the phone, others only through your personal visit.

• **Credentials.** Some resume companies advertise size, longevity and/or $6, $7 and $8 resumes. Resume quality is more important than price or company size. What you are looking for is proof that they produce effective professional resumes that open doors. Ask for client references, not just samples.

After an initial consultation the writer should be able to advise you on the best type of resume. Yes, there are several. The most common is the **chronological,** and it's fine if you have an uninterrupted work history and wish to remain in the same field. However, if you have been a job hopper, are just entering the work force following schooling, or if you are over 40, changing career fields, returning to the work force after a divorce, military retirement or raising a family, the **functional,** (sometimes called the targeted or skills format) or the **hybrid** are far more effective.

• **Appearance.** Your resume provides the prospective employer with his or her first impression of you. Although typewriter-generated resumes are quite acceptable, I strongly recommend your final resume be prepared on desktop publishing.

> Here is a simple comparison of the type quality difference. The newer electronic typewriter can provide **bolds,** *italics* and even different type sizes, but none compare in appearance to the type that can be generated by a personal computer word-processing program.

• **Price.** Although a consideration, cost is secondary to other factors. As I mentioned earlier, you can expect to pay between $50 to $150 for a professional resume and cover letter. In most cases you will definitely want to include a cover letter with your resume. *Often it is more important than the resume itself.*

Most writers will be reluctant to quote a firm price on the phone. They will likely give you a range. To a large extent, the fee depends on two factors: 1) completeness of the information you provide; and 2) length or complexity of the resume. Remember a resume is not a work of fiction...it is your work history. No one can provide that except you. You can hire the best tax preparer in the world, but he can do nothing until you provide the necessary information. The more information you provide and the better it is organized, the less time it will take to put into form. Just as you are billed by an attorney, accountant or psychologist, you are paying for the professional writer's time. After an initial free consultation, you should be provided a fee quote.

Note: I have included worksheets in Appendix 3 that will help you prepare and organize your work history information.

Some offices may attempt to sell you on a fancy four-page "brochure" layout with prices as much as $300 or more. Not only is this an unnecessary expense, but according to my research, most personnel officers prefer the standard 8 1/2" by 11," printed on either white or off-white bond. Your resume should be one or two pages. The exceptions to this rule are few and primarily limited to those professionals with many years in a highly technical or scientific field. Even here, this technical information is best placed as an addendum to the resume.

Assuming you possess the required job qualifications, the keys to a door-opening resume are:

- Remember your resume is a *marketing tool* not a *career obituary.* It should clearly *identify the benefits* your prospective employer will receive by hiring you.
- Your resume should *focus on your future,* not on your past.
- It should summarize your *accomplishments...not job duties.*
- It should *document skills you enjoy using,* not things you did because you had to.
- Appearance should be neat and uncluttered with plenty of white space.
- Brevity, consistent clear organization, and ease of reading are all keys.

THE COVER LETTER

In most cases you will want to introduce your resume with a cover letter. I *strongly* recommend that each cover letter be an original addressed to the individual who will be reviewing your resume. A generic cover letter will be quickly identified as part of a mass mailing and is far less effective.

I suggest two options:

> • If you have your resume, cover letter and letterhead prepared on desktop publishing equipment, supply your preparer with a disk and ask for a copy. Your cover letter can then be quickly and inexpensively retrieved to insert the salutation, thus providing an original cover letter on matching letterhead for each prospective employer in minutes.
>
> • A second option is to prepare a sample cover letter that you can then customize on your own typewriter. Be sure to type it on your matching letterhead, which was prepared along with your typeset resume. In either case, the letterhead and stationery for your cover letter should match the resume.

The four basic ingredients of a good cover letter are:

1. Grab the reader's attention with quality letterhead stationery. As mentioned, it should match your resume, both in type face and in paper. By matching your cover letter and resume, you give an impression of balance, continuity, and professionalism. Basic business letters should be laid out according to accepted standards. *(See samples in Appendix 2.)*

2. Generate interest with the content. You do this by first addressing the letter to the reader by name and quickly explaining the reason for your letter, the specific position/type of work you are seeking, and from which resource (help-wanted ad, referral, etc.) you learned of the opening. Be direct and confident.

Note: When making your initial telephone contact, be sure to check your key contact's name, correct spelling, pronunciation, title, and verify the address and phone number.

---

3. Next, turn that interest into desire. Summarize your pertinent background and refer the reader to the particular credentials on your resume that are relevant to your candidacy.

Then indicate why you are interested in the position/company/ products/services. Stress what you can contribute to the company.

4. Turn the desire into action by asking for an interview. Emphasize your desire for a personal meeting and your intention to follow up your letter with a phone call. *Then do it!*

A professional resume writer will be able to prepare a powerful cover letter......*but you must supply the custom information,* such as company name, key person, address and zip.

Sample resumes and cover letters have been included in Appendix 1 and 2.

"A Hunting We Will Go"

• ...Putting it all Together

Method...

"We often get in quicker by the back door than the front."

...Napoleon

"He who does nothing renders himself incapable of doing anything; but while we are executing any work, we are preparing and qualifying ourselves to undertake another."

...William Hazlitt

"The world is sown with good; but unless I turn my glad thoughts into practical living and till my own field, I cannot reap a kernel of the good."

...Helen Keller

GATHERING AND
ORGANIZING THE INFORMATION

Now that we have all the pieces, let's put them together.

Assuming you have your resume and general cover letter, or they are in process, you should go to the library to develop your prospecting list. Even though I have explained the process, when you have the directory in front of you it may seem a little over-whelming, so let's review.

- First check the "How to Use This Directory" section. Most will use either the Standard Industrial Code, (S.I.C.) or the yellow pages format. If you have any questions about listings or how to locate the one(s) you are looking for, *ask the librarian.*
- Armed with this organizational information, turn to the appropriate section. Here you have the complete business listings you need for your prospecting.

Since directories are reference books, you can't check them out. So with pencil in hand and a stack of 3 x 5 cards, copy the information on your cards. Place only one business on each card. *You'll see why in a minute.* I suggest this information be placed uniformly on each card. For example, always place the firm's name in the upper left, telephone upper right, etc. The more business listings you gather, the better. I recommend you begin with at least 100 firms.

When you have your stack of completed cards, it is time to go home, put on a pot of coffee and start the qualifying. At this step you'll understand the reason you used cards instead of a sheet of paper to gather your prospects.

At home, find yourself a roomy work space. The kitchen table is fine. You'll be dividing your prospecting cards into three or four piles or groups by priority. First prepare three or four header cards marked "Choice #1," "Choice #2," etc. Each priority group should consist of at least 25 businesses. The "Choice #1" stack should con-tain the businesses you would most prefer to pursue.

Identifying priorities will be different for each person. Your first priority may be location. It may be firms you know, or firms known to pay well. Whatever your priorities, arrange your cards under your priority header cards. Then place a rubber band around each stack. Time now for a break and a cup of coffee. You've earned it. You won't start your *Kitchen Table Direct Contact Prospecting* until tomorrow.

KITCHEN-TABLE PROSPECTING TO LAND THE INTERVIEW

There are good reasons for starting your direct contact campaign as early as possible in the morning:

- You are more likely to find the key contact you wish to talk with in his office.
- You are normally rested and more mentally alert.
- Typically you and your key contact are less likely to be distracted at this time of the day.

Now that you have your prospect cards organized you are ready to begin.

Go after what you want with high intention, determination and commitment. Know you are good and don't be afraid to project that image to the person on the other end of the conversation!

REMEMBER...
The Primary Objective of Your Call is to:
- Establish personal contact with the decision-maker.
- Locate job openings that can be followed up with your resume and personalized cover letter.
- Arrange an interview appointment.

Start with the "Choice #2" and "Choice #3" stacks. The reason for starting here is for practice. You have far less to lose by "messing up" with firms from these stacks than in the "Choice #1" stack. After a few calls you will learn what to expect and develop a strategy for handling different situations. When you feel more comfortable, move to "Choice #1."

Before Dialing Each Firm:

- Review the information on your prospecting card.
- Have in mind what you want to say to your contact. Something that will interest him or her...along with why your resume and requests should be considered.
- Smile.....it will put a smile in your voice.

A typical call might go something like this:

Secretary:	*"May I tell him who is calling?"*
Answer:	*"Yes, this is James Allen."*
Secretary:	*"May I tell him the nature of your call?"*
Answer:	*"I am doing some research on employment opportunities in the (science, computers, telecommunications) industry and wish to speak with Mr. Smith personally."*

Be prepared to experience a lot of "sorry, but..." . Steel yourself for it and remember a "sorry, but..." is *their loss...not yours.* You can expect to receive 10, 20 or more "no openings" before getting a "yes." And believe it or not, a "no" can be the best answer of any...if you ask the most important question before hanging up.

When you are given a referral, and you will, often, you have the *key* to *positioned* or *power prospecting*. The referral may not know you but he will surely know the person who referred you. Any salesman will tell you a known referral almost always turns into a sale. This is why super stars like Michael Jordan, Bo Jackson and Michael Jackson earn more for their endorsements than from their professions.

Following each call, make brief notes on your card regarding the conversation. Now prepare four more header cards. "Submit Resume," "Interview Scheduled," "Maybe," and "No." When you get a "Yes" to your request to submit your resume or for an interview, place that card under the appropriate header card for follow-up action. It is also wise to have your calendar handy (included in Appendix 3) and immediately note the appointment date, time, firm, person, title and phone number for each scheduled interview. You don't want to run the risk of conflicts.

Continue each direct contact session for about two hours. It will be tiring and you don't want that fatigue to show in your voice and/or manner.

After each session take your "Submit Resume" stack and prepare your custom cover letter and enclose it with your resume. Be sure to double-check your spelling and address on both the cover letter and envelope. You might wish to pick up a "Confidential" rubber stamp at your office supply and stamp each envelope. It gives your letter a connotation of importance and it will stand out from others in the morning stack of mail. I recommend using a 9 x 12 white envelope. *It will be remembered!*

Follow-up: Keep good records of when each letter went out and call the recipient *five* days from the date you mailed it. This will time your call for approximately the day after your resume has been received. *Make these calls on schedule. They are critical to your interview campaign.*

Wow...you've done it! You have learned how to locate the huge "hidden job market" and, more importantly, how to turn it into a *direct contact*. Statistics show the *direct-contact* method will produce twice as many interviews as any other.

Continue to work the advertised jobs too, but you now have the skills to locate 80 in the "hidden market" for every 20 in the classifieds. And believe me, there will be far less competition for that "hidden" 80. In short, it means more opportunities, more interviews, more offers and more options.

Well, I believe that brings us full circle. Now let's review...

SUMMARY

Once you have your resume and cover letter prepared, you can do all of your prospecting and follow-up from the comfort of your kitchen table. Not only will this method place you at the front of the line, but you'll uncover that vast reservoir of the available jobs others will never know exist.

- Arm yourself with a professional resume.
- Research the appropriate directories for your prospects and prepare a file card for each applicable listing. *(See Appendix 4)*
- At home you can *qualify* your prospect listings according to *your* priorities, such as location, personal knowledge, company size, etc.
- Then begin your telephone prospecting campaign to locate those job opportunities that will never appear in the classifieds. Practice with "Choice #2" or "Choice #3" stacks first.
- Get past the receptionist to your key contact. Be sure to verify your contacts name, title, spelling and address for your cover letter.

- Follow up each positive response by mailing your resume and a *customized cover letter* within 24 hours.
- Five days after mailing your resume, call the person to whom you mailed your resume to make sure it has been received. This would also be a good time to inquire about what action, if any, has been taken and when you might expect an interview. *Handled properly, this call will:*
    - Remind your contact of your name.
    - Reinforce your sincere interest in their job opening.
    - Stimulate action...!

Now you have the *Professional's Secret to Locating All the Job Openings*....not just the advertised 20 percent. Combine this 80-percent advantage with the direct-contact method of landing the job interview and you have the most comprehensive and efficient keys to getting that job you are looking for.

REMEMBER

...You Don't have to be Good to Start
BUT
You Have to Start To Be Good...

...You've earned your license...
...HAPPY HUNTING

P.S. ...DON'T OVERLOOK APPENDIX 4.
...Sources and Resources...

This listing is the key to your local research!

The Employment Interview ... Setting the hook

- Key traits employers always look for
- Anatomy of an employment interview
- Typical interview questions
- Suggested answers for the tough questions
- Interview protocol:
    - *...Guidelines for a successful employment interview*

THE ANATOMY OF AN EMPLOYMENT INTERVIEW

Wow! At last you have reached the final step – the job interview. You've set your goals, developed your network, prepared the cover letters, resumes and thank-you notes, located and prioritized potential employers, done your kitchen-table job prospecting, located openings and submitted your resumes. Now you have been invited for the job interview. You need to know what to expect and what is expected.

One of the best ways to prepare is through practice. Remember how you prioritized your 3 x 5 cards under those firms you would most like to work for, those that would be your second, third and fourth choices? I suggest you do the same thing here.

Practice interviews are like pre-season games. If possible, it is best to build your interviewing skills with companies low on your priority list. You will note a growing sense of confidence with each interview.

In the employment interview you want to provide information about yourself that demonstrates you would be a valuable and productive member of the organization. At the same time, the employment interview provides you with an opportunity to obtain specific information about the job and the organization in which you are interested. This information will be very important later if you are offered the job. You must gain information about a job and the organization that wants to hire you before you can make an informed decision whether to accept or reject a job offer.

Getting the Answers You Need

During the employment interview, you should do more than just answer questions. You should use this time to get answers to the questions you have concerning the job you are considering. You will get answers to some of your questions (such as whether you think the work environment will suit you) indirectly from what the interviewer says and through your observations. Other questions should be addressed directly. Effective interviewers will give you plenty of time to ask questions. Make sure you are prepared with some questions you would like answered. For example, any of the following questions are appropriate during an employment interview.

- What are the specific duties and responsibilities for the job?
- What are the training and educational opportunities?
- How have those who have had this job in the past done in the organization?
- What are the organization's future plans and goals?
- What are some examples of the best results produced by people in this job?
- What exactly would you like to have me accomplish in this position?
- Do you have any questions about my qualifications?
- How soon will you make a hiring decision?

The Screening Interview

Usually there will be two or more interviews prior to a hiring decision. The first, the "screening interview," typically is the most difficult. Here the interviewer's job is to reduce the number of applicants to a "short list." In larger companies the screening interview is typically conducted by a staffing interviewer in the human resources or personnel department. This interviewer often has only sketchy information about the specifics of the job. He or she is gathering data, both objective and subjective, regarding your general qualifications and is looking for reasons to eliminate you.

Remember the screening interview is not designed to hire, but to eliminate candidates.

Objective data includes appropriate degrees, skills and experience. Often, tests will be given to check skills such as typing speed, computer and software literacy, etc.

Subjective conclusions are drawn from both your verbal responses, and your nonverbal behavior. Nonverbal messages are communicated by such things as the way you are dressed, your eye contact, posture, etc.

(See Guidelines for a Successful Job Interview below.)

This is where the **CEED** in our word **SUC-CEED** is demonstrated

---

C = **Confidence** - *Objective and Subjective*
  - Do you sound intelligent?
  - Do you exhibit any obvious emotional disturbances?
  - Are you articulate?
  - Are you a positive person?

E = **Experience** - *Objective and Subjective*
  - The right degree?
  - The right experience, skills?

E = **Enthusiasm** - *Subjective*
  - Sufficient enthusiasm and energy for the position?

D = **Dedication** - *Subjective*
  - Do you truly want this job?
  - If hired, will you be responsible and loyal to this employer?

Warning: It is during the screening interview that you are most likely to encounter the worst possible test, the *stress interview.* Let's examine it briefly.

The Stress Interview is more likely to be encountered if the position is one requiring supervision and/or decision-making responsibilities. The key is to recognize it for what it is, and react accordingly.

First understand this is not a personal attack. It is an exercise to ascertain how you conduct yourself under pressure. *There is nothing personal intended! The purpose is to make you feel confused, fearful and hostile.*

The stress interview is easy to recognize and is characterized by:

- Questioning your credentials.
- Sarcastically soliciting reasons why you feel your training and experience make you qualified for this position.
- Questions are rapid fire, and jump from one topic to another. Sometimes your interviewer interrupts you with a totally unrelated question.

Now that you understand what is going on, you can handle it like a pro.

- *Recognize the situation for what it is* – an artificial scenario designed to see how you react under pressure. The interviewer has nothing against you personally.

- *Stay Calm.* Never take your eyes from the interviewer. When he/she finishes asking a question, take a second to compose yourself...then answer.

- *Don't get angry or despondent.* Remember, the stress interview is designed to see if you will become depressed, hostile and frustrated when the going gets tough.

- *Watch your tone of voice.* It's easy to become angry or sarcastic during a stress interview. Some unsuspecting candidates even break into tears.

By recognizing the stress interview and understanding its purpose and intent, you can display the calm, perceptive, level head they are searching for.

Typical Employment Interview Questions

1. Tell me about yourself.
2. How would you describe yourself?
3. Have you done this type of work before?
4. Why are you interested in working here?
5. Why are you interested in this job?
6. What do you know about our organization?
7. Why did you leave your last job?
8. What are your salary requirements?
9. What was your salary at your last job?
10. Why would you be better for this job than someone else?
11. How many days a year did you miss at your last job? Why?
12. Do you have any physical limitations that would prevent you from doing this job?
13. When would you be available to start if you were selected?
14. What are your major strengths?
15. What are your major weaknesses?
16. How do you compensate for your weaknesses on the job?
17. What are your immediate employment goals?
18. What are your long-term employment goals?
19. You seem over/under-qualified for this position. Why do you want this job?
20. How long do you plan on keeping this job if you get it?
21. What kinds of machines and/or equipment can you operate?
22. What have you been doing since you left your last job?
23. Have you ever been fired? Why?
24. How did you get along with your co-workers, supervisor, clients and/or customers in your last job?
25. What kind of people do you work with best?
26. What kind of work environment do you prefer?
27. What did you enjoy *most* about your previous job?
28. What did you enjoy *least* about your previous job?

29. What were your typical duties in your previous job?

30. Why are you looking for a new job?

31. What would you ideally like to do?

32. How do you feel about pressure, deadlines, travel, relocating, overtime or week-end work?

33. What makes you lose your temper?

34. What do you like to do in your spare time?

35. To what type of managerial style do you respond best?

36. For what type of organization do you want to work?

37. What would you like to accomplish if you were hired for this job?

38. Give me an example of your creativity, problem-solving ability, initiative, willingness to work hard, reliability.

39. What are the toughest problems you have faced and how did you handle them?

40. What kinds of decisions are most difficult for you?

41. What have you learned from your previous work experience?

FEED INFORMATION INTO THE CONVERSATION THAT POSITIVELY REFLECTS YOUR DESIRE TO BE CONSIDERED FOR THE JOB.

Some Response Guidelines for the Tough Interview Questions

Employers usually ask questions that fit into these broad categories and can be responded to as follows:

Questions employers want answered:	How you respond... Points you want to make:
Why did you choose this organization?	You have done your research and can speak knowledgeably about the organization, its goals and how these goals match yours.
What can you do for me? (Benefits:)	You know what the organizational needs are and how you can meet them.
Have you done this kind of work before?	Respond with brief, to-the-point descriptions of how a skill you used before relates directly to the employer's needs.
Will you fit in here?	The employer may be concerned about your fitting in with your co-workers, taking directions or coping with a hectic pace. Mention briefly and in a positive way the jobs where you worked in these situations.
How much will hiring you cost me?	Ask for a salary range. Your salary should be related to your experience and skills.

	(Some suggested sources for researching this question would be help-wanted ads, other employers and/or employment agencies.)
Tell me about yourself.	Employers want to gain information about your work experience, not your personal life. Talk about experiences that relate to the specific job for which you are applying.
How would you describe yourself?	Discuss positive work-related attitudes. For example, you might suggest that you enjoy working with people, are loyal, committed, etc.
Have you done this type of work before?	Link the skills you possess to the abilities needed. Answer truthfully about how your experience relates to the position.
(• Older workers might be asked something like...) "We don't have many employees here that are your age. Would that bother you?"	Emphasize that you are still anxious to learn and improve and that it doesn't matter who helps you.

INTERVIEW HINTS

- Think of the interview as an adventure rather than a tribunal, and try to enjoy it. A positive rather than fearful attitude will allow your mind to perform at its best.

- **Be enthusiastic** about the position and about your accomplishments; about what you've found out about the company and the job for which your are interviewing.

- **Be honest.** Express enthusiasm only about the things you are genuinely enthusiastic about. Phoniness will not sell the hiring manager or the screening interviewer on you.

- **Keep on smiling.** Sure, you're accustomed to giving people a big smile when you shake hands with them. In the interview, keep on smiling. A smile makes you appear agreeable and pleasant
     ...and who wouldn't want to work with a pleasant and agreeable person like you?

- **Make lots of eye contact.** When someone doesn't look you in the eye you begin to wonder what that person has to hide. Make eye contact while you're shaking hands with the interviewer and *frequently* throughout the interview, *but...*

- **Don't stare** or make continuous eye contact – *that would make anyone feel uncomfortable.*

- **Be positive.** It's best to keep negative words out of your interview vocabulary to the extent possible. *You must put a positive spin* on such issues as your reasons for leaving, relations with your superiors, etc. When rehearsing your answers to interview questions, *take all the negative words out.*

- **Be confident enough and prepared enough to take control of the interview if need be.** Don't let the hiring manager's lack of interviewing skill or preparedness keep you from shining. In most cases the unskilled hiring manager will thank you for the help. Remember, you are just the person he/she is looking for...help them recognize that you have that "certain something" that will help them....

Suc-CEED

Final Preparations: Last-minute check list before leaving for the interview:

- Call to confirm the interview time.
- Know the interviewer's name, title and phone number.
- Know the organization's address and have directions for getting there. Make a practice run before your interview.
- Make sure your appearance in appropriate.
- Take with you:
  - a couple of pens
  - your application form notes
  - two copies of your resume
  - your list of references
- Make sure you arrive at least 10 minutes before your interview is scheduled so you can relax and feel comfortable with your surroundings before you get started with the actual interview.

After the Interview

After an employment interview you should do the following:

- Within 24 hours of the interview, send a thank-you note.
- Call the interviewer regarding his/her decision at the time specified in the closing of your interview.
- If you are told that you did not get the job, try to find out why. Emphasize that if any similar positions come open within the organization, you would still be interested in working for them. Also ask the interviewer if he/she could recommend any other organizations that you might talk to about the kind of job you are considering.

- Offers: *I want you to get several employment offers.* These offers become bargaining or negotiating chips. Just like an auction, a competing offer can be used to negotiate a higher starting salary, benefits, perks, etc.

As a rule of thumb, even when you get an offer you wish to accept, *never do so on the spot.* Tell the employer you are interested in his/her offer and wish to consider it. Be sure to set an agreed-upon time limit, for acceptance; i.e. by noon Wednesday. Here again, the practice interview becomes a very valuable learning experience.

GUIDELINES FOR A SUCCESSFUL JOB INTERVIEW

APPEARANCE

This is the first thing on which the employer will judge you.

- Plan your interviewing wardrobe carefully.

Women
Keep your dress simple, neat and attractive. Your own taste and the latest fashion may not be the best guideline. A conservative approach will always be considered professional and acceptable with employers. A navy-blue suit is a safe, appropriate interview uniform.

- Choose accessories, shoes and handbags that compliment your outfit. Jewelry should be kept to a minimum.
- Hair should be clean and shiny; never worn in an extreme style.
- Perfume should be worn at a minimum, or not at all.

- Make-up is an asset to most women; however, don't be guilty of heavy, obvious make-up on an interview. A clean natural look is the most pleasing.

Men

A conservative business suit, tie and shirt is always appropriate. Follow other appropriate conservative, business grooming customs.

BE PREPARED

- Arrive a few minutes early. **NEVER BE LATE!** If anything happens to delay you, telephone the company and advise them you will be late. If you find you cannot make the interview due to circumstances beyond your control *contact the company immediately.*

- When you go on your interview, *go alone.* **Never take children or a friend.**

- Take with you the following:
    - Two copies of your resume, which includes a list of names, dates and addresses of past positions and references.
    - If you do not have a resume, make certain you have this necessary information with you for completing an application:
        - Social Security Card
        - Pen
        - Perhaps a Pocket Dictionary
        - Birth Certificate

- Check your appearance before you enter the office. Then settle down, relax take a deep breath and think positive thoughts. *Remember, this is a great adventure...not an inquisition!*

- If you have gum, throw it away and *don't smoke in the office.*

- Make sure you remember the duties of the job you are interviewing for, what the company does and what they are looking for in an employee for this position.

- Be prepared to answer questions such as: "What do you feel you can offer to our company?" and "What sort of a position would you like to be in three to five years from now?" These are difficult questions if they have not been given previous thought prior to the interview. Gear your answers to what the company is offering and traits they wish for this position.

FILLING OUT AN APPLICATION

- Fill out in detail. Be careful with your spelling. A misspelled word can cost you the job.
- Write or print legibly and neatly. Follow directions carefully.
- If you were let go from a previous position, it would sound much better to say "laid off" rather than "fired." In most cases a simple explanation will suffice, if the interviewer questions you on this. *Never, speak disrespectfully of your previous employers. Remember Thumper's mother's advice,.....* "If you can't say something nice – don't say anything at all!"

THE INTERVIEW

- Enthusiasm and a smile will many times outweigh background and experience in an employer's selection. Remember this!
- Acknowledge the interviewer's introduction, always using his/her name during the interview.
- Introduce yourself, with a firm handshake and a smile. Remember, first impressions are usually lasting.
- Sit down when you are invited to; use the chair your interviewer indicates.
- Place your purse or briefcase beside your chair, never on your interviewer's desk.
- Fold your hands in your lap. Don't play with jewelry, keys, hair, etc.
- Sit erect, but be relaxed.
- Maintain eye contact with your interviewer without letting your eyes wander....*but do not stare.*
- Speak clearly and in your normal tone of voice. The interviewer must be able to hear you. Don't be bashful or pushy. Be friendly.
- Let the interviewer guide the conversation. Don't interrupt with your own questions. There will be time for these.
- Answer all questions in a straightforward, friendly manner, using discretion when necessary. *Never answer with simply a "yes" or "no".* Explain when possible.

- Stress only positive feeling during the interview. Never imply negative or bitter feelings, especially in regard to former employers. This will only hinder you.

- *Do ask questions.* Employers like to know you are interested. This is a compliment to them.

- Sell yourself by stressing your ability and your desire to learn.

- Never assume the employer knows you want the job. He/she may be waiting for you to indicate your interest. If you want the job – *ask for it!* You can say something like, "I would like to work for your company." Or "Would you consider hiring me? I know I would be a good employee." Or "If offered, I would accept this position."

- Accept competition gracefully. There may be other applicants for the job, so don't be discouraged if he/she asks you to wait for a decision.

- Thank him/her personally and leave gracefully and quickly when the interview is over.

- Send a thank-you-letter within 24 hours. Restate your interest and how you will make a major contribution

- Now if you do not feel that you are interested in the job, **never turn down a job offer on the interview or indicate negative feelings.** If you are in doubt, ask him/her if you can give it some thought and call later. Once you have indicated negative feelings during an interview, the employer will no doubt not consider you, even if you decide the next day you want the job. It is always best to think it over, and talk with your spouse or a trusted friend first.

Study these guidelines thoroughly. You will save yourself much valuable time in obtaining a job.

...The Resume...

- Basic Formats
- Handling Problem Circumstances
- Examples

* See Bibliography of Resume Books-Appendix 3

APPENDIX 1....THE RESUME

Have you been wrestling with your resume because you perceive unfavorable or unusual circumstances in your professional or educational background? Or maybe you are at a loss as to how to capitalize on certain strengths. Believe me, you are not alone. Most people face some kind of challenge in developing a resume that will present them in the most favorable light.

Remember: Your Resume is a *sales* piece, not a *career obituary*. It needs to *bristle with benefits* for the employer.

Earlier I mentioned there are several types of resume formats. Each format is designed to organize and present your unique circumstances in the most powerful and persuasive way.

Basic Resume Formats

Chronological format. Work experience and personal history are arranged in reverse time sequence. This format is the most traditional and is fine if you have consistent professional growth in a single career or profession. *It will not be advantageous, however, if you are just out of school, have experienced numerous job changes or prolonged periods of unemployment.*

Functional format. Work experience, skills and abilities are catalogued by major areas of involvement. This format focuses on your professional skills and abilities rather than duties and time chronology. *This is a better format for the new graduate, career changer, displaced homemaker or mom returning to the work force after raising children, early retiree, or the older worker.*

(With variations, the functional format is sometimes called a targeted or skills format.)

Hybrid Format: Combines elements of both the chronological and functional formats. In today's job marketplace, I feel this format offers the advantage of spotlighting your "benefits" right upfront as *Highlights of Qualifications.* Such a format seems to be gaining popularity with employers. Like the functional format, it focuses on what you *can* do, rather on what you *have done.*

Note: It is wise to have your resume(s) prepared on desktop publishing. By placing your resumes on a disk, you can easily and inexpensively tailor each resume to highlight those areas of greatest importance to each prospective employer.

Example 1 • **All employment in one company**
Demonstrates excellent career growth within the firm by highlighting each position held and the responsibilities assumed in that position.

Example 2 • **Career change or applying for jobs in related fields**
Utilizes the "Objective" as a career target, highlighting transferable skills from past jobs.

Example 3 • **Business owner reentering the job market**
Here is an appropriate format for reentering the job market.

Example 4 • **Wish or need to de-emphasize earlier employment**

Example 5 • **"Job hopper"**
Demonstrates a de-emphasis of the numerous listings by omitting descriptions of previous employment.

Example 6 • **Over 40 or have gaps in employment**
Concentrates on qualifications, skills and achievements rather than actual dates of employment.

Example 7 • **Military background**
Translates military jargon into accepted business terminology.

Example 8 • **Student or new graduate**
Emphasizes education and related activities to demonstrate competence.

Example 9 • **Moving from temporary employment into the job market**
De-emphasizes "temp" image by listing actual company names rather than the agency name and eliminates short-term dates of employment.

Example 10 • **How to stress need for confidentiality**

Example 11 • **Retirement from civil service to pursue a totally different field**
Hybrid Resume format used to highlight acquired and transferable skills.

Example 12 • **All employment in one company**

...See Examples on the following pages...

Example 1 Shows increasing responsibility within one company. See Example 12 as well.

STEVEN G. SECURITY
12 Protection Road
Boston, Massachusetts 02100

Residence: 617/ 000-0000   Business: 617/ 000-0001

QUALIFICATIONS:

- Certified Protection Professional.
- 14 years progressive management experience in security operations.
- Accountability in finance, marketing, operations, and administration.
- Established network of clients in high tech, medicine, and education.
- Hands-on experience in physical security, audits, and inspections.

EXPERIENCE:

FGE SECURITY SERVICES CORPORATION   BOSTON, MA
(New England-based contractor of security personnel • 10th largest in U.S. • 2800 employees)

District Manager - Boston, MA   **10/87 to present**
(Direct a staff of Operations, Human Resources, Training, and Audit Managers in delivery of services
to 20 major high-tech accounts within highest producing 128/North Shore territory • 350 employees
• $10M budget)

District Manager - Boston, MA   **2/86 to 10/87**
(Directed a staff of Operations, Human Resources, Training, and Audit Managers in delivery of services to
14 medical and educational institutions in the Longwood Medical Area • 300 employees • $6M budget)

Director of Operational Audits & Inspections - Boston, MA   **1/85 to 2/86**
(Corporate responsibility for the financial and operational management of 25 Audit and Inspection personnel)

Regional Manager of Operational Audits & Inspections - Boston, MA   **6/84 to 1/85**
(Regional responsibility for the financial and operational management of 7 Audit and Inspection personnel)

Area Manager - Boston, MA   **2/80 to 6/84**
(Directed 7 supervisors in the delivery of services to 7 commercial accounts • 125 employees • $1.5M budget)

Facility Supervisor - Boston, MA   **2/77 to 2/80**
(Operational responsibility for the uniformed security services at St. Francis Hospital and Medical Center)

Shift Supervisor / Security Officer - Boston, MA   **12/74 to 2/77**
(Supervisory responsibility for the uniformed security services at St. Francis Hospital and Medical Center)

EDUCATION:

EBR University - School of Law Enforcement and Security   Boston, MA
Bachelor of Science Candidate in Security Administration (52 credits)

CERTIFICATIONS:

AMERICAN SOCIETY FOR INDUSTRIAL SECURITY
Certified Protection Professional   1987

INTERNATIONAL ASSOCIATION FOR HOSPITAL SECURITY
Hospital Security Officer   1976

References available upon request

Example 2 Utilizes the Objective as a career target; highlights transferable skills from past jobs.

NEIL NEW DIRECTION
61 Versatile Avenue
Boston, Massachusetts 02100
617/ 000-0000

OBJECTIVE:	Entry-level position in Human Resources.	
EDUCATION:	JHU STATE COLLEGE	BOSTON, MA
Dec 84	Bachelor of Science in Education, cum laude Major: Elementary Education Minor: Social Welfare	
EXPERIENCE:	VMN ELEMENTARY SCHOOL	BOSTON, MA
Sep 86 to present	**Grade Six Teacher** • Wrote and implemented Science curriculum. • Designed Student Council program. • Presented materials to School Committee. • Conducted meetings with professional and educational colleagues. • Representative to state convention for Boxford Teachers Association. • Authored monthly parent correspondence.	
	KJM & COMPANY	BOSTON, MA
Sep 84 to present	**Security Assistant** • Responsible for daily security operations. • Directed departmental safety and loss prevention systems.	
	FTE SCHOOL	BOSTON, MA
Sep 85 to Jun 86	**Grade Seven Teacher** • Taught Math, Science, Social Studies. • Organized school athletic programs. • Implemented extracurricular activities.	
	YMCA	BOSTON, MA
Jan 83 to Jun 84	**Program Director** • Oversaw daily functioning of after-school day-care program. • Supervised staff of summer day-care programs. • Coordinated overall management of 90 children enrolled in program.	
	EDF MARKET	BOSTON, MA
Sep 79 to Sep 82	**Manager** • Managed 50 employees. • Handled employee-management relations. • Maintained financial records.	

REFERENCES FURNISHED UPON REQUEST.

Example 3 Business owner reentering the job market, or needing a resume for a client or business plan.

Melvin F. Marketing
19 Promotional Way
Boston, MA 02100
617/ 000-0000

MARKETING / OPERATIONS MANAGEMENT

Professional Experience:

MFM ENTERPRISES • Boston, MA   1986 to present
Principal. Direct the efforts of three marketing specialists in the development of marketing recommendations and operational solutions for leading N.E. residential/commercial real estate companies.

- Conduct market surveys to determine market penetration and evaluate other geographical areas for possible market expansion. Recommend changes in advertising strategy and company marketing literature.
- Select and install office microcomputers. Coordinate the design, development and implementation of computerized property appraisal analyses and client/customer data bases.
- One client increased market share by 5% in 4 months and was recognized as #1 multiple office franchise in New England. Company plans included expansion into three new marketing areas based on recommendations.

GHT INC.
INFORMATION SYSTEMS DIVISION • Boston, MA   1982 to 1986
Marketing Manager (1984 to 1986). Directed four senior product managers and two application engineers in the management of major product programs accounting for 15% of total company sales ($75M).

- Introduced comprehensive computer-based system within 14 months of initial design. Test site culminated in a $24M commitment.
- Increased sales by $2.25M within six months by introducing a unique product into untapped market segment.
- Eliminated uprofitable product with $500K annual savings.
- Closely collaborated with engineering to formulate project priorities, cost estimates and schedules.
- Developed effective professional relationships with key industry decision-makers.

Industry Marketing Manager/Senior Product Manager (1982 to 1984). Developed and implemented market and product strategies for numerous product lines and market segments.

- Introduced the company's first multi-user, multi-tasking minicomputer.
- Directed efforts to determine application strategies.
- Supervised the preparation of product requirements and product introduction plans.
- Represented company at regional and national trade shows and conventions.

FRT COMPANIES INC. • Boston, MA   1962 to 1982
Operations Manager (1978 to 1982). Directed a 16-member department in the research and assessment of new procedures, equipment, and automated techniques for implementation company-wide.

- Coordinated the company's conversion to store computerization resulting in its commitment to a $30M chain-wide conversion based on success with initial system.
- Justified above endeavor with a 28.82% average R.O.I. over five years based on a leasing approach.
- Achieved productivity savings of $7.4M annually through chain-wide computerization.

Received rapid promotions through Management and Operations positions (1963 to 1978).

Education:

SWE UNIVERSITY • Boston, MA
Bachelor of Science in Business Administration   1970
CONTINUING EDUCATION AND IN-HOUSE SEMINARS
Marketing and Management
REAL ESTATE SALES LICENSE

Example 4 The focus is on present professional status; entry-level only listed.

Sales
Marketing
Public Relations

ALICE ACCOUNT REP

91 Quota Road   • Boston, Massachusetts 02100 • (617) 000-0000

Experience:

SENIOR ACCOUNT REPRESENTATIVE
IYUJ INC. • Boston, MA   1988 to present

Develop new advertising customers and renew established accounts in a
north-shore territory. Consistently meet or exceed monthly quotas.
Outperform all other rookie reps. Received rapid promotion in company's
career track toward Major Account Rep.

MANAGER OF OFFICE LEASING
SALES BROKER
THE OLI COMPANY • Boston, MA   1985 to 1988

Directed planning and day-to-day operations of Office Leasing Division
for this high-end commercial real estate brokerage. Devised and
implemented successful marketing plans in a soft market.

Contributed to the planning, design and production of collateral materials
to support a new corporate name and image. Conducted market research,
developed copy, and collaborated with graphic design, photography, and
printing professionals to produce the final products.

Independently prospected for office leasing/sales business. Acquired
exclusive listings on land and office buildings in a highly competitive
market. Marketed and presented listings to developers and investors. Sold
94-acre tract of land, the largest sold by company in 1987. Managed
company-owned office building.

Actively participated in city-wide public relations functions. Member of
the Business Inquiry Committee of the Greater Boston Chamber of
Commerce. Assisted in the Industrial Development Research Council
1987 World Congress for Corporate Facility Planners.

LICENSED REAL ESTATE BROKER
HYT/RFT, INC. • Boston, MA   1982 to 1985

Earned numerous Recognition Awards for Top Ten Sales Performance.

REAL ESTATE SALES ASSOCIATE
YHJ AND COMPANY • Boston, MA   1980 to 1982

Education:

BACHELOR OF ARTS IN JOURNALISM
THE UNIVERSITY OF BOSTON • Boston, MA   1980

Specialized in News and Urban Affairs with course emphasis on public
relations, marketing, advertising and reporting. Interned as P.R. Asst. for a
retail mall and Reporter/Copy Editor for college newspaper.

TOM HOPKINS SALES COURSE

POWER COMMUNICATION SKILLS

Example 5 Explains reasons for job change and de-emphasizes numerous listings by omitting job descriptions.

JEANNE JOB HOPPER
Box 000
Boston, Massachusetts 02100
617/ 000-0000

SUMMARY

Successful professional record encompassing marketing support, inside sales, and customer service • Solid communication skills • Demonstrated ability to manage simultaneous projects and meet deadlines • Strong organizational and problem-solving ability • Computer experienced.

PROFESSIONAL EXPERIENCE

Administrative Manager • TJA • Boston, MA   2/91 to 2/92

- Supported Marketing Development Manager in the preparation and production of product literature for trade shows and sales presentations. Assisted in the implementation of corporate identity materials with new company name and logo.
- Provided administrative support to the International Marketing Department during Manager's extensive travel. Furnished international dealers with appropriate distributorship agreements, data sheets, and brochures.
- Directly supervised temporary support staff.

Position was eliminated due to departmental reorganization.

Inside Sales Representative • PS Inc. • Boston, MA   12/89 to 9/90

- Supported outside sales force in the management of East Coast high technology accounts.
- Established efficient methods to compile/maintain sales data and administer paperflow.
- Wrote and edited newsletter released to established and prospective customer base.

Position was eliminated due to economic considerations.

Service Coordinator • BDS • Boston, MA   2/89 to 12/89

- Coordinated network of representatives in the servicing of nationwide accounts.
- Resolved customer problems/technical inquiries and doubled dollar value of service contracts.
- Assisted in marketing research on newly released product.

During company strike, recruited by PS, Inc. President.

Office Manager • DCS, Inc. • Boston, MA   8/88 to 2/89

Credit Manager • BBS • Boston, MA   5/87 to 7/88

EDUCATION

Bachelor of Arts in English with Biology background
HCK COLLEGE • Boston, MA   1986

References available upon request

Example 6 An excellent format for older candidate. Concentrates on qualifications, achievements and years in each position rather than actual dates of employment. Also excellent format for covering gaps in employment history.

Alice M. Administrator   4 Solid Terrace, Boston, Massachusetts 02100 617/ 000-0000

Summary of Qualifications:
- Seasoned administrator in both business and academic environments with expertise encompassing program development; staff recruitment, orientation, training, and evaluation; office management; budget preparation; grant writing; and public relations.
- Solid teaching and training background.
- Strong communication, negotiation, organization, and problem-solving skills.
- Demonstrated capability managing simultaneous projects and successfully meeting deadlines.
- Active leadership in a variety of community organizations.

Employment Highlights:
EDUCATIONAL ADMINISTRATOR • Public Schools • Boston, MA   (7 years)
- Established initial guidelines, budgets, and staffing for the local implementation of a federally sponsored public education program.
- Wrote and submitted proposals and amendments to obtain federal and state grants.
- Recruited, trained, supervised, and evaluated staffs.
- Promoted programs within the community through the preparation and dissemination of information.

OFFICE MANAGER • KLI Insurance Agency Inc. • Boston, MA   (1 year)
- Managed administrative operations of a full-service insurance firm including accounts receivable, accounts payable, correspondence, and customer service.
- Utilized word processing and accounting software packages on PC.

PERSONNEL RECRUITER • JVF Electronic Systems • Boston, MA   (2 years)
- Recruited, hired, trained, and internally placed all non-technical staff.
- Provided orientation for exempt and non-exempt employees.
- Established and implemented a technical typing/secretarial training program.

Education/Training:
MASTER OF ARTS IN PSYCHOLOGY • NBH University • Boston, MA
BACHELOR OF SCIENCE IN PSYCHOLOGY • LKN College • Boston, MA

Related Activities:
BOARD OF DIRECTORS • Boston Council of Social Concern   (3 years)
Executive, Personnel, and By-Law Committees.

BOARD OF DIRECTORS • Boston Citizen Advisory Board   (3 years)
Selection Committee.

CAMPAIGN MANAGER • Boston Board of Selectmen Candidates   (2 years)

Example 7 An excellent example of a functional resume format. It shows how military jargon is translated into accepted business terminology.

FRED M. FUNCTIONAL   2252 Detailed Avenue, Boston, MA 02100

OFFICES: 617-000-0001; 617-000-0002   HOME: 617-000-0000

PLANNING AND OPERATIONS MANAGEMENT

SUMMARY

More than twenty years of progressively responsible management positions in complex, diversified organizations. Extensive hands-on experience in organizational structuring, strategic planning, policy development, professional education and telecommunications operations. Strong, persuasive writing and presention skills that convincingly articulate organizational goals, objectives and direction.

MANAGEMENT

Currently Assistant Deputy Director for Information Systems of a large Federal Agency with operations at eleven US and four overseas locations. Previous experience as Director of Operations for a specialized agency responsible for national-level training management. Drove major organizational changes to include functional consolidations and spin-offs based on technical state-of-the-art. Integrated and coordinated diverse actions to assure consistency with organizational goals and objectives.

PLANNING

Spearheaded development of the US Army post-1990 Training Estimate and related national-level studies and analyses. Devised specific telecommunications contingency plans for short-notice, high-risk national operations to include the US civilian evacuation of Nicaragua and contributed to the development of similar plans for Lebanon and Iran. Designed and coordinated the telecommunications portion of joint programs to test and validate relevant plans and initiatives.

POLICY

Directly contributed to the development of US national telecommunications policy affecting both strategic and conventional operations. Proposed US Army national training goals and objectives and contributed to related national policy and program initiatives. Authored US Army worldwide training standardization policy. Articulated policy initiatives as speechwriter for top-level officials.

OPERATIONS

Managed and directed telecommunications line organizations responsible for operations and maintenance of US communications facilities in Korea, Vietnam and Saudi Arabia to include telecommunications centers, telephone exchanges, secure voice terminals, high frequency radio stations and telephone outside plants. Implemented modernization program for facilities in Saudi Arabia and initiated plans for subsequent expansion.

EDUCATION

Bachelor of Arts, LJU University, English-Journalism
Master of Science, RFT University, Political Science

CLEARANCE

Top Secret (Special Background Investigation)

PERSONAL

Completing service in the US Army with grade of Lieutenant Colonel.

Example 8 Emphasizes education and education-related activities to demonstrate scholarship and competence.

STEPHANIE STUDENT

Advertising and Marketing

15 Wishful Drive • Boston, Massachusetts 02100 • 617/ 000-0000

EDUCATION

degree:	**Bachelor of Science in Business Administration** *(concentration: Marketing)*
	IKJ STATE COLLEGE 1992
honors:	Dean's List.
coursework:	Marketing Management, Marketing Research, International Marketing, Advertising.
activities:	Marketing Society, American Marketing Association.
projects:	**Marketing Research.** Member of team that researched utilization patterns of the BUV State Park by tourists and local residents. Interviewed employees, investigated guest book entries, and surveyed local residents. Presented oral and written findings.
	Advertising. Member of team that devised a 6-month print and radio advertising campaign for an area bakery. Collected and analyzed all pertinent financial and marketing data, determined target markets, and developed appropriate advertising budget. Presented oral and written findings.
	Business Policy. Conducted extensive research into the positioning of YHU Groceries in the marketplace. Interviewed corporate president and reviewed financial and management data, and analyzed strengths and weaknesses of proposed buy-out. Generated comprehensive report of analyses and conclusions.
internships:	**The College.** Created and designed advertisements in a weekly college newspaper for local retail businesses. Closely collaborated with sales and graphics staff. Increased customer accounts. Gained experience on various typesetters.

EMPLOYMENT

Sales Assistant.	
YTB's • Boston, MA	1990 to 1991
Gymnastics Teacher.	
RECREATION DEPARTMENT • Boston, MA	1985 to 1990
Waitress.	
BUV STATE PARK • Boston, MA	1991 to 1992
H&J's • Boston, MA	1988 to 1992

References available upon request

Example 9 De-emphasizes "temp" image by listing actual company names rather than the agency name; eliminates short-term dates of employment.

TRICIA TEMP
8 Variety Road • Boston, Massachusetts 02100
617/ 000-0000

SUMMARY OF QUALIFICATIONS:

- Strong administrative background within a variety of demanding environments, including high technology, engineering, construction, and consumer.
- Solid secretarial skills, including business & technical typing, editing & proofreading, word processing, dictaphone, meeting planning, reception, and switchboard.
- Proven ability to interact effectively with clients and staff at all levels.
- Proficient in handling simultaneous projects and meeting deadlines effectively.

EMPLOYMENT:

Temporary   *1983 to present*

ABC • Boston, MA • Executive Offices and Human Resources Department.

DEF • Boston, MA • Productivity Review Engineering Department.

GHI • Boston, MA • MIS and Human Resources Departments.

JKL • Boston, MA • Engineering/Sales/Quality Assurance Departments.

Permanent   *1958 to 1983*

MNO COMPANY • Boston, MA
Sales Assistant/Designer Clothing (1977 - 1983).

INDEPENDENT COLOR CONSULTANT • Boston, MA
Certified Consultant (1970 - 1977). Assisted business professionals in enhancing personal style in order to achieve professional goals.

PQR COMPANY • Boston, MA
Secretary/Sales Department/Household Products Division (1965 - 1970). Supported District Sales Manager, Group Managers, and sales representatives in the areas of product specials, new product availability, competitive pricing, test marketing, and meeting planning.

STU ENGINEERS • Boston, MA
Administrative Assistant (1962 - 1965). Provided liaison with Inspector of Naval Material to expedite clearance investigations and applications for technical interim employees.

VWX CONSTRUCTION COMPANY • Boston, MA
Payroll Clerk (1958 - 1962). Calculated withholding taxes and union dues for personnel on job sites.

EDUCATION:

Continuing Education • Public Speaking, Marketing, Achieving Management Potential

Diploma, HYU High School • Boston, MA   1957

ASSOCIATIONS:

Professional Secretaries International • *Women of Boston* • *Fundraiser, Knights of Columbus*

Example 10 Stressing confidentiality when looking for a new position while still employed.

Confidential Curriculum Vitae
of
STANLEY J. SUPERINTENDENT

566 Student Avenue   Residence: 617/ 000-0000
Boston, Massachusetts 02100   Office: 617/ 000-0001

SUMMARY:

- Seven years of significant contributions as Assistant Superintendent (K-12) in Boston, Massachusetts.
- Proven ability to lead an experienced teaching/administrative staff with vision, flexibility, and sensitivity.
- Demonstrated expertise in fiscal management, collective bargaining, long-range planning, staff development and evaluation, program development, and grant writing.
- Strong commitment to positive, dynamic relationships with community and government organizations.

EXPERIENCE:

Assistant Superintendent of Schools (K-12)
BOSTON, MASSACHUSETTS   1980 to present
(3,700 student enrollment • 350 professional and paraprofessional staff • $16M budget)

Highlights:

MAJOR CONTRIBUTOR TO POLICY / BUDGET PLANNING AND ADMINISTRATION.

PERSONNEL ADMINISTRATION *(Recruitment, Supervision, and Evaluation)*

- Recruit and evaluate 6 Principals, Director of Computer Applications, and Director of Science Resource Center.
- Contribute to evaluation of teachers, other administrators, and instructional aides.
- Collaborate in contract negotiations, collective bargaining procedures, and arbitration hearings. Successfully facilitated 1980 reduction-in-force of 56 personnel with minimal disruption.
- Currently initiating and coordinating a comprehensive staff transfer program in order to promote increased job motivation, productivity, and satisfaction.

PROGRAM DEVELOPMENT *(School and Community)*

- Administered reorganization of plant, staff, and programs to meet the needs of significantly reduced high school population.
- Initiated an ongoing Alcohol Task Force Advisory Group comprised of educators, clergy, and business leaders. Task Force implemented a chapter of Students Against Drunken Drivers (SADD), peer education programs, and a town-wide awareness week.
- Established new Alternative Education Program for high school students.
- Obtained teacher training grants from Governor's Alliance Against Drugs and Alcohol & Highway Safety Bureau.
- Contributed to the design of a community-wide Foreign Exchange Student Program.

CURRICULUM DEVELOPMENT *(Model Programs)*

- Elementary Science Resource Center.
- Concepts of Peace - a collaborative effort with Educators for Social Responsibility.
- Health Education - prevention of AIDS and substance abuse.

Coordinator of Secondary Education
BOSTON, MASSACHUSETTS   1971 to 1980

Highlights:

- Implemented the middle school concept, successfully spearheading the simultaneous transition to a new high school and two middle schools.
- Established a "team" organizational structure including all major disciplines and guidance to improve the scope and coordination of educational programming.
- Led professional staff in the development of basic skills and curriculum guides in all disciplines.
- Launched dynamic PTO's at both the high school and middle school levels.
- Established network of paraprofessionals.

Senior Supervisor in Education
Assistant to the Associate Commissioner for Curriculum and Instruction
BOSTON DEPARTMENT OF EDUCATION   1969 to 1971

Research Associate
NEA CENTER FOR THE STUDY OF INSTRUCTION   1966 to 1969

High School Social Studies Teacher
BOSTON, MASSACHUSETTS   1967 to 1969
UYT, MARYLAND   1963 to 1967

EDUCATION:

Critical Thinking Institute
LYU. UNIVERSITY   Summer, 1987

Teacher Evaluation and Merit Pay
AASA INSTITUTES   1986

Post-graduate work in Curriculum and Instruction (30 credits)
UNIVERSITY OF RTE   1969 to 1972

Master of Arts in History
SDR UNIVERSITY   1969

Bachelor of Arts in History and Education
UTB UNIVERSITY   1963

CERTIFICATIONS:

Massachusetts Certificate # 0000: Superintendent/Assistant Superintendent (K-12), Principal (7-12).

CONSULTING POSITIONS:

- *Public Schools* of Brookline, Orange, Stoughton, Ipswich, Dighton-Rehobeth, Reading, Mass., and Leonia, NJ. Shawsheen Valley Technical & Vocational School.
- Scholastic Editorial Advisory Board
- NEA Center for the Study of Instruction
- Merrimac Education Center
- Excellence Program for Massachusetts Schools

STAFF DEVELOPMENT ACTIVITIES:

Legal Issues in Education

Simulations in the Classroom

Performance Objectives and the Individualization of Instruction

Value Clarification and Problem Solving

Social Studies in Open-Space High Schools

Opening the Elementary Classroom

Performance Objectives in the Elementary Social Studies Classroom

Team Teaching and the Individualization of Instruction

Basic Principles of Curriculum Development and Evaluation

The Development of Interdisciplinary Learning Packages

Current Trends in Curriculum Development

Mainstreaming

Alternative Career Planning for Educators

The Development of Individual Behavioral Objectives for IEP's under Chapter 766

Basic Skills Improvement Programming

Career Education

Curriculum Mapping

PROFESSIONAL AFFILIATION:

President, Massachusetts School Executive Association

Life Member, National Education Association

American Association of School Administrators

Association for Supervision and Curriculum Development

National Association of Elementary Principals

Phi Delta Kappa

References available upon request

Example 11 Hybrid resume format used to highlight acquired and transferable skills following retirement.

KENNETH C. MAESTAS

0000 Zang Way • Golden, Colorado 80000 • (303) 000-0000

Objective: Position as Commercial Art Illustrator or Cartoonist specializing in caricatures.

Highlights of Qualifications
- Creative and artistic sense in graphic design and caricatures.
- Keen observer, learn quickly, interpret information accurately.
- Highly motivated self starter; enjoy accomplishments whether independently or as a team.
- Proven skills in graphics including page layout, overlay and key production, color composition, airbrush and color illustrations through color markers and various paint medias.

RELEVANT EXPERIENCE

Print Media
- Designed book cover, created and prepared camera-ready cover and text illustrations for *How To Pick a Dandelion*, by Marion Hart Pratt, Published by Angel Press.
- Prepared illustrations for the Montgomery Alabama Public Library "Read-a-thon".

Logo Design
- Designed and created camera-ready logo art used by:
  - Denver Police Federal Credit Union.
  - Barber Ammunition.
  - Shear Art Hair Design.

Cartoon and Caricature
- Developed and created cartoons for the Police Union Publication.
- Designed artwork for silkscreened T-shirts.
- Numerous commissions to create caricatures.

Leadership and Communication
- As a veteran Police Officer have acquired and demonstrated:
  - Responsibility, reliability and competence working independently or as a team member in dealing with daily requirements.
  - Developed oral communication skills working with the public, supervisors and fellow officers including court room testimony.
  - Proven written communications through documenting official reports and logs, as well as correspondence on criminal activities and commendations to citizens.

WORK HISTORY

1972 - Present	The Denver Police Department	Denver, CO
1970 - 1971	United States Army	

EDUCATION

- Colorado Institute of Art   Denver, CO
  - 1990 Associate Degree of Occupational Studies in Visual Communications
    - *Awards:* Honor Roll
- Rocky Mountain School of Art   Denver, CO
- Denver Police Academy   Denver, CO

Portfolio and references available upon request

Example 12 Another hybrid format example showing progressive and increasing responsibility within one company.

TERRY L. CONSISTENT

777 South Lincoln • Denver, CO 80010 • (303) 783-1111

Objective: A challenging management position with a reputable construction firm. One in which my progressive and comprehensive experience in construction would be utilized to meet the corporate mission. The ideal position will allow opportunities for continued professional growth, autonomy and responsibility.

HIGHLIGHTS OF QUALIFICATIONS

More than 15 years experience in all phases of construction and supervision including:

• Supervision of entire construction project from survey through completion.
• Responsible for quality control of each phase.
• Writing specifications, bidding, purchase of materials scheduling of subcontracting.

Certification

• Construction Supervisor Class B; Aurora, CO, Denver, CO, Colorado Springs, CO

PROFESSIONAL CONSTRUCTION EXPERIENCE

Estimating and Bidding
• Accurately and profitably estimated building projects from survey to finish.
• Successfully estimated all subcontracting including plumbing, heating, electrical, sheetrocking, roofing and concrete .

Contract Planning and Scheduling
• Developed contract language documenting agreed-upon prices, schedules, procedures and responsibilities.
• Reviewed plans and developed schedules with architects, contractors and subcontractors assuring proper coordination, efficiency and profitability.

Coordinating and Subcontracting
• Successfully supervised and coordinated all work crews including specialty subcontractors.

Job Control and Building Inspections
• Assured subcontractors' strict adherence to projected scheduling and costs.
• Achieved consistent high quality control in compliance with building codes and inspection standards.

Final Project Wrap-up
• Completed detailed pickup work on all projects, achieving extremely high level of client satisfaction, consistently generating new referrals and repeat business.

EMPLOYMENT HISTORY

1972 to present	Colorado Commercial Builders,	Denver, CO
• 1981 to present	Construction Supervisor	
• 1977 - 1981	Assistant Supervisor	
• 1975 - 1977	Carpentry Foremen	
• 1973 - 1975	Carpenter	
• 1972 - 1973	Laborer	

EDUCATION

Iowa State University   Ames, IA
Major: History

References and Portfolio available upon request

APPENDIX 2

...The Cover Letter...

- 13 Examples for Various Circumstances
- The Thank-You Letter

APPENDIX 2 – THE COVER LETTER

Before writing your cover letter, it is wise to do some homework on each company. You can find background information in your library. This can be done either during your initial "prospecting" or after you have made your telephone contacts and have requests for your resume.

In addition to your local directories, I recommend you also check publications such as the *Dun & Bradstreet Directory* and *The Thomas Register* along with state-wide directories of manufacturers and service industries. You may also find company annual reports and newsletters; trade journals; and company public relations departments helpful as well.

Ask your librarian for assistance. He/she will be happy to help. Additionally your librarian can direct you to other valuable resources I have not included here.

Just as there are resume formats for dealing with differing circumstances, the same holds true for cover letters. *Sample letters for each of these circumstances are provided.*

Examples 1 & 2	• Following your phone call
Examples 3 & 4	• Career change
Example 5	• Layoff
Example 6	• Mass mailing
Example 7	• Recent graduate
Example 8	• Recruiting agency
Examples 9 & 10	• Reentering the job market
Examples 11 & 12	• Referral
Example 13	• Thank-you letter...
	Don't overlook this letter. It should always be sent following your interview!

If you have had your resume prepared by a professional resume writer, you may also want him or her to prepare the appropriate cover letter(s). Another option is to have a *general* cover letter professionally written as a guide. You then may individually personalize and type it on your letterhead to fit each circumstance. Check prices first!

Note: *For the highest degree of professionalism, your cover-letter stationery should match your resume. If you have your resume professionally prepared, request matching letterhead as well.*

As a final reminder: Never underestimate the power of a well-written personalized cover letter! *It might make the difference between getting that interview or not.*

Example 1 Following a phone call. Typed on typeset letterhead.

Susan L. Burke
_____

11 Lorraine Terrace • Boston, Massachusetts 02100   617/ 000-0000

June 15, 1993

Ms. Stephanie Morehall
LKY Corporation
32 Concord Avenue
Boston, MA 02100

Dear Stephanie:

I enjoyed talking with you about the marketing position you have open in the customer support area. After you have had a chance to review the enclosed resume, I would like to meet with you and further discuss my qualifications for the job.

It is my belief that customer service and support are the most important factors in keeping customers and building additional business. My success in selling can be largely attributed to my service orientation. In the past, I have thought that many companies for which I have worked could have increased sales if they had also provided services that maximized the use of their products. It would be very interesting to me to become involved with researching and implementing various customer support services.

The skills I have acquired while selling would be very beneficial in this type of marketing position. Having worked in the field, I know what customers need and how to uncover those needs. In addition to my selling skills, my analytical skills have been sharpened through my MBA program. As I sold turnkey systems in the high-tech marketplace, I am confident that the transition to the typesetting market would be a smooth one.

I will be in touch with you by the end of next week to arrange for a convenient meeting time. Thank you for your consideration.

Sincerely,

Susan L. Burke

Encl.: resume

Example 2 Following a phone call. Typed on plain paper.

5 Franklin Street
Boston, MA 02100

July 15, 1993

Ellen Richards
Recruitment Coordinator
L-P-D
1 Clarendon Street
Boston, MA 02100

Dear Ms. Richards:

Thank you for forwarding informational materials describing career
opportunities at L-P-D. It was interesting to learn about the impressive scope
of services that L-P-D provides its clients and the many programs it offers its
employees to encourage their professional growth and development.

Enclosed please find a current resume in support of my application for a
position as an Assistant Actuary.

I hold a Bachelor of Science Degree in Economics with a concentration in
Finance. Since 1986 I have worked as an Account Controller at the State
Street Bank and as a Labor Market Economist for the state Department of
Employment and Training. Both positions required strong quantitative,
analytical, and research skills.

I am able to work independently under deadlines, am highly motivated, and
can communicate effectively at all levels. My success as an amateur hockey
player has demonstrated my discipline, energy, and desire to work hard and
excel.

I would welcome an opportunity to discuss my qualifications and the
possibility of future employment with L-P-D. I look forward to hearing from
you at your earliest convenience.

Sincerely,

Donald Fitzgerald

Encl: resume

Example 3 Career change. Typed on plain paper.

61 Arcadia Avenue
Boston, MA 02100

Aug. 15, 1993

Ms. Linda Scott
Human Resources Manager
JKL Enterprises
43 South Street
Boston, MA 02100

Dear Ms. Scott:

Enclosed please find a current resume in support of my application for an
entry-level position in Human Resources at JKL.

My background includes a Bachelor of Science degree and several years
experience in teaching and educational program management. While I have
thoroughly enjoyed my career and am proud of my many accomplishments, I
am seeking a new direction that offers greater challenge and financial
growth potential.

From my research of business operations, I am convinced that the heart of
any organization is its Human Resources Department, and it is an area
where I feel I can readily make a contribution. My strengths are in training,
oral and written communication, interpersonal skills, planning and
organization, attention to detail, ability to learn quickly and adapt to new
situations, and the capacity to perform well under pressure.

I would welcome an opportunity to discuss my qualifications and the
possibility of future employment with JKL. I will contact your office next
week to determine the feasibility of setting up a personal meeting at your
earliest convenience.

Sincerely,

John Caban

Encl: resume

Example 4 Career change, noting source of reference. Typed on plain paper.

120 Tremont Street
Boston, MA 02100

Sept. 15, 1993

Mr. Dan Meade
Dean, Business Department
FGH College
342 Fisher Avenue
Boston, MA 02100

Dear Mr. Meade:

At the suggestion of Ellen Kole, I am enclosing a current resume in support of my application for a full-time teaching position at FGH College.

While I am probably not the traditional candidate, I bring a combination of an accounting degree, diverse business expertise, and a lifelong interest in a career in education.

After fifteen years as the owner and president of a profitable textile business, it was my decision to close the company and pursue a variety of other business/teaching endeavors. For example, I currently consult to start-up textile companies to establish or improve their production and material sourcing. I am also the sole owner of a self-storage company. In addition, I am the portfolio manager for a large profit sharing account and trust fund.

The most enjoyable part of my career now is teaching Accounting I at FGH College, and I hope to use this experience and my business expertise to launch a full-time teaching career. I am confident that my educational background and practical business experience would enable me to enrich the curriculum in management, marketing, economics, and accounting theory. In addition, my textile/design background would allow me to design practical projects geared both to design students and business majors.

I would welcome the opportunity to further discuss my qualifications and how I might make a contribution to the business programs at FGH College. I can make myself available for a personal interview at your convenience and look forward to hearing from you.

Sincerely,

Ken Merchant

Encl: resume

Example 5   Cover letter following a layoff. Typed on plain paper.

7 Muriel Road
Boston, MA 02100

Oct. 15, 1993

Trevor Winston
Director of Personnel
GJY Insurance Co.
113 School Street
Boston, MA 02100

Dear Mr. Winston:

Enclosed please find a current resume in support of my application for the position of Customer Service Manager as advertised in the Boston Globe.

Currently I hold the position of Supervisor of Customer Service, Underwriting Records at Mutual Insurance Co., where I supervise 12 people in the maintenance of customer records. I was recruited to this position from Computer-Plus Corporation, where I was the Supervisor of Data Entry for nearly 10 years.

While I thoroughly enjoy my affiliation with Mutual Insurance Co. and am proud of the increase in departmental productivity under my direction, the company is presently under receivership. This unfortunate circumstance necessitates that I seek an alternative position where I can continue to utilize my strong organization, planning, problem-solving, and supervisory skills.

Your advertisement particularly interests me because my research has indicated that GYJ is an industry leader and expanding in Greater Boston. I am confident that I am a strong candidate for this position because I am experienced in all aspects of customer service operations in an insurance setting.

I look forward to further discussing my qualifications and how I can contribute to GYJ. I will contact you next week to explore the possibility of setting up a meeting at your earliest convenience.

Sincerely yours,

Sandra Feldman

Encl.: resume

Example 6 Mass mailing cover letter. Note that this is addressed to a specific person and hides the fact that it is a mass mailing. This will prove more productive than addressing, "Personnel Director," "Sirs," etc.

18 Irving Street
Boston, Massachusetts 02100

Nov. 15, 1993

John Taymore
Vice President
TGB Ltd.
95 Eldred Avenue
Boston, MA 02100

Dear Mr. Taymore:

I am interested in exploring the availability of positions in Product Management at TGB.

My background includes a Masters in Business Administration as well as seven years developing, producing, and marketing products used by electronic component manufacturers.

Presently I am employed as a Product Manager/Development Chemist at BVC Company, a recognized leader in the production of specialty chemicals. My responsibilities include the planning and management of projects through research, qualification, manufacturing, and sales introduction as well as the exploration and commercialization of new technologies and products. Not only do I ensure high-quality products, but also outstanding service and product training.

I am confident that my unique background, encompassing technical, management, and marketing expertise, qualifies me to greatly contribute to the continued success of your product development program.

I would welcome the opportunity to further discuss my qualifications and learn more about any available positions at TGB. I will call you next week to determine whether it is possible to set up a meeting at your earliest convenience. However, should you desire to reach me before that time, please feel free to do so at either number listed on my resume.

Sincerely yours,

Phillip J. Payson

Encl.: resume

Example 7 Recent graduate. Typed on plain paper.

11 Irvine Street
Boston, MA 02100

Dec. 15, 1993

Ms. Sarah J. Rodriguez
Vice President
The Boylston Company
Farley Place
Boston, MA 02100

Dear Ms. Rodriguez:

Enclosed please find a current resume in support of my application for a position as a Mutual Fund Performance and Business Analyst at The Boylston Company. I have researched The Boylston Company and learned about the excellent available opportunities through Mr. James Chin, an employee at your subsidiary, The Boylston Safe Deposit and Trust Company.

As a Finance major at Boston College, I acquired strong analytical, quantitative, research and writing skills coupled with a working knowledge of PC's, financial software packages, and business operations. My coursework included Financial Analysis, Financial Policy, and Accounting.

I am able to work independently, am highly motivated, and can communicate effectively. My background as a world-ranked figure skater and continued activity related to that sport have demonstrated my discipline, energy, and desire to work hard and succeed.

I would welcome an opportunity to discuss my qualifications and the possibility of future employment with The Boylston Company. I look forward to hearing from you at your earliest convenience.

Sincerely,

Sharon Emerson

Encl: resume

Example 8 Cover letter written to a recruiting agency.

5 Euclid Avenue
Boston, MA 02100

July 15, 1993

Jean-Yves Pierrat
FGT Corporation
43 High Street
Boston, MA 02100

Dear Mr. Pierrat:

As we previously discussed by telephone, I am forwarding you a current resume in the hope that your firm might be helpful in securing me a management position in the hotel industry.

I hold an Associate of Science Degree in Hotel and Restaurant Management and most recently worked for Durham Hotel and Resorts as a Front Desk Manager in both Columbia, S.C., and Los Angeles, Calif. I have established a solid record for both my knowledge of hotel operations and my ability to run an efficient, cohesive organization. I am particularly aware of the necessity for a well-trained, highly motivated staff in order to achieve company goals.

The following information might also be useful to you in placing me:

1. I am primarily interested in a position in the Boston area, but would consider relocation within New England.

2. My salary expectation is $25K+, with important considerations being benefits, location, and growth potential.

3. Two references to contact at the Columbia Durham in Columbia, S.C. (803/ 000-000), are Steven Stone, General Manager and Connie Hope, Restaurant Manager.

If you need further information, please feel free to contact me days or evenings at 617/ 000-0000. I look forward to a productive working relationship with your organization.

Sincerely yours,

Laurie R. Silverberg

Encl.: resume

Example 9   Reentering the job market.

2 Elmwood Avenue
Boston, MA 02100

Aug. 15, 1993

Ms. Lillian Belden
Office Manager
Brosnan & Johnson
23 Commercial Way
Boston, MA 02100

Dear Ms. Belden:

Enclosed please find a current resume in support of my application for the position of Paralegal as advertised in Legal Weekly.

I completed Paralegal Studies at MCT College in 1986 and have solid experience working in a general law office. I recently returned to Boston from New York and Connecticut and am temporarily employed in the Corporate Law Offices of the Bank of Middlesex.

Although relatively new to this career, I bring with me extensive legal knowledge coupled with maturity, enthusiasm, and a wealth of life experience.

While raising a family, I pursued diverse and interesting activities including owning an antique shop, serving as a general contractor on a private residence, and spearheading many successful community fund-raisers. Now that my children are adults, I am seeking to channel all my energies into a paralegal career.

I would welcome the opportunity to further discuss my qualifications and learn more about your law firm. Please feel free to contact me at either telephone number listed on the enclosed resume.

Sincerely,

Susan H. Brown

Encl.: resume

Example 10 Reentering the job market. Typeset letterhead enhances professional presentation.

RHONDA RICH   49 Russell Road   • Boston, MA 021000   • 617/ 000-0000

Sept. 15, 1993

Ann Stevens
RDW University Office of Career Services
33 Trowbridge Street
Boston, MA 02100

Dear Ms. Stevens:

Enclosed please find a current resume in support of my application for the position of Business Counselor as advertised in the Boston Sunday Globe.

I hold Masters degrees in both counseling and education and have worked in diverse environments including established and start-up businesses, education, and medical settings.

In 1982 I founded and have since operated a one-person career consulting business, whose services are outlined in the enclosed literature and include testing, counseling, resume preparation, video-taped interview practice, and workshops. Business has prospered at a remarkable rate and recently I have been approached by a prospective buyer who has made a serious offer. Therefore, I am exploring alternative career options in the same field. Your advertisement seemed a perfect match.

I would welcome the opportunity to further discuss my qualifications and how I might contribute to RDW's career programs for students and alumni. Please feel free to contact me days or evenings at the above telephone number.

Sincerely yours,

Rhonda Rich

Encls.

Example 11 Referral cover letter.

Beth Harris Evans

25 Highland Avenue
Boston, Massachusetts 02100

(617) 000-0000

Oct. 15, 1993

Brian Spind
Director of Production
WEEE-TV
23 Boston Avenue
Boston, MA 02100

Dear Mr. Spind:

At the suggestion of our mutual friend Mary Jones, I am writing to inquire
as to available production positions at WEEE-TV. My background and interest
lie particularly in the area of educational programming and I plan to enter a
Master of Education program in the fall in order to pursue a long-term goal
in educational television.

Most recently I worked for five years as an Associate Producer and
Audio/Video Manager at a major Boston advertising agency. During this time
I planned and produced award-winning television commercials for both local
and national clients. For your convenience I have enclosed a current resume
and video portfolio that feature many of my projects there.

I am now interested in broadening my experience in film and video by
seeking out a new challenge in television. WEEE-TV particularly interests me
because of the quality of programs it produces and funding it attracts.

I would welcome the opportunity to further discuss my qualifications and
how I could contribute to your production team at WEEE-TV. I will contact
your office next week to determine the possibility of setting up a personal
meeting at your earliest convenience.

Sincerely yours,

Beth Harris Evans

Encls.

Example 12 Referral cover letter. Same as Example 11 except this letter has been typeset. You will note how this enhances the professional appearance and can be very effective in setting your cover letter and resume apart from others.

Beth Harris Evans

25 Highland Avenue
Boston, Massachusetts 02100

(617) 000-0000

Nov. 15, 1993

Brian Spind
Director of Production
WEEE-TV
23 Boston Avenue
Boston, MA 02100

Dear Mr. Spind:

At the suggestion of our mutual friend Mary Jones, I am writing to inquire as to available production positions at WEEE-TV. My background and interest lie particularly in the area of educational programming and I plan to enter a Master of Education program in the fall in order to pursue a long-term goal in educational television.

Most recently I worked for five years as an Associate Producer and Audio/Video Manager at a major Boston advertising agency. During this time I planned and produced award-winning television commercials for both local and national clients. For your convenience I have enclosed a current resume and video portfolio that feature many of my projects there.

I am now interested in broadening my experience in film and video by seeking out a new challenge in television. WEEE-TV particularly interests me because of the quality of programs it produces and funding it attracts.

I would welcome the opportunity to further discuss my qualifications and how I could contribute to your production team at WEEE-TV. I will contact your office next week to determine the possibility of setting up a personal meeting at your earliest convenience.

Sincerely yours,

Beth Harris Evans
Encls.

Example 13 The all-important thank-you letter. Again, if you type on plain paper, it should match your resume stationery.

54 Forest Street
Boston, MA 02100

Dec. 15, 1993

Mr. David Walsh
President
P&E Associates
57 Allied Drive
Boston, MA 02100

Dear Mr. Walsh,

I enjoyed meeting with you on July 28 and very much appreciated the generosity you showed by readily taking time from your busy schedule to talk with me at such an early hour.

It was extremely informative to discuss with you the different aspects of the growth of P&E Associates. I am very interested in joining your organization in a Domestic Sourcing management capacity and would welcome the opportunity to add to your continued success.

Thank you again for your time and interest in me. I look forward to hearing from you if an opening materializes in the near future.

Sincerely yours,

Linda R. Fallon

...Your Worksheets...

- Priority Grid
- Priority Grid Sample
- Job History Outline
- Job History Worksheets
- Basic Skills Check List
- Action Verbs Word List
- Personality Profile Word List
- Scheduling Calendars

PRIORITY GRIDS

A Priority Grid can be a very helpful tool, not only for ranking your daily activities, or "Do List" and keeping you on track, but also for helping you make important decisions.

Here are just a few sample applications:

> • Set goals (daily, weekly, monthly, annually, or even lifetime)
> • Identify and/or rank your "likes" in a:
>   • job
>   • work environment
>   • friends
>   • relationships
> • Prioritize your values or your skills
> • ...even a vacation itinerary

Whenever options present themselves, your priority grid will help you make sense out of chaos. I'm sure you will be amazed as you apply this simple method to any list of options or choices.

As a test run, just try it on a list of 10 things *you like to do.* If you're like most people, you will find they don't always stack up the way you might have guessed. For example, I thought fishing was my favorite leisure activity only to find there were several others I actually ranked higher.

On the next page is a sample priority grid with instructions for use. Then I have included an original form and suggest you make at least 10 or 15 copies for your use. *Don't write on the original as you will probably want to make additional copies as you exhaust your original supply.*

Take a little time to work with your sample priority grid. I think you will find it very valuable...not only in your job search but as a personal time-management and decision-making tool on a daily basis.

PRIORITY GRID SAMPLE

Each day we have a number of things that we wish or need to accomplish. A key factor in getting things done is wise management of time. This grid will help you do just that...here's how.

(1) The first thing you need to do is write tasks/items down as they come to mind. This is done in random order. This can be done anytime. I generally make my list in the evening or while enjoying my morning coffee.

(2) After you have your list, it then needs to be ranked by *current importance* to you. By starting with the highest priority items and working down your list you are always working on the most important items. Don't worry about completing each item on your list. I seldom do. Unfinished items can be carried ahead to the next day. Notice that priorities can and do change daily! The value of listing and prioritizing is that you are using your time in the most effective manner, accomplishing tasks that are most important first.

Items To Be Ranked

1.	6.
2.	7.
3.	8.
4.	9.
5.	10.

Compare the items on the previous page, one pair of items at a time. Pick ONE for EACH of the pairs, and circle your choice below. When you can't decide, just pick one; it will come out in the wash.

1 or 2   1 or 3   1 or 4   1 or 5   1 or 6   1 or 7   1 or 8   1 or 9   1 or 10

2 or 3   2 or 4   2 or 5   2 or 6   2 or 7   2 or 8   2 or 9   2 or 10

3 or 4   3 or 5   3 or 6   3 or 7   3 or 8   3 or 9   3 or 10

4 or 5   4 or 6   4 or 7   4 or 8   4 or 9   4 or 10

5 or 6   5 or 7   5 or 8   5 or 9   5 or 10

6 or 7   6 or 8   6 or 9   6 or 10

7 or 8   7 or 9   7 or 10

8 or 9   8 or 10

9 or 10

Now summarize below. Count up and enter below – how many times did you circle #1?, #2? etc.

#1___ #2___ #3___ #4___ #5___ #6___ #7___ #8___ #9___ #10___

When there's a tie look back and see which from that pair, you chose earlier, and rank it higher.

Copy the items over again, but now list them in the order of *their priority* (for today).

Final Ranked Order

1. _____   6. _____

2. _____   7. _____

3. _____   8. _____

4. _____   9. _____

5. _____   10. _____

PRIORITY GRID:

*Publisher grants the reader permission to copy this form for personal, non-commercial use.

Items To Be Ranked

1. _____   6. _____
2. _____   7. _____
3. _____   8. _____
4. _____   9. _____
5. _____   10. _____

Compare the items above, one pair of items at a time. Pick *one* for *each* of the pairs, and circle your choice below. When you can't decide, just pick one; it will come out in the wash.

"Quickies" - Misc.

1 or 2   1 or 3   1 or 4   1 or 5   1 or 6   1 or 7   1 or 8   1 or 9   1 or 10

2 or 3   2 or 4   2 or 5   2 or 6   2 or 7   2 or 8   2 or 9   2 or 10

3 or 4   3 or 5   3 or 6   3 or 7   3 or 8   3 or 9   3 or 10

4 or 5   4 or 6   4 or 7   4 or 8   4 or 9   4 or 10

5 or 6   5 or 7   5 or 8   5 or 9   5 or 10

6 or 7   6 or 8   6 or 9   6 or 10

7 or 8   7 or 9   7 or 10

8 or 9   8 or 10

9 or 10

Now summarize below. Count up and enter below. How many times did you circle #1?, #2?, etc.

#1____ #2____ #3____ #4____ #5____ #6____ #7____ #8____ #9____ #10____

When there's a tie look back and see which from that pair, you chose earlier, and rank it higher.

Copy the items over again, but now list them in the order of their priority (for today).

Final Ranked Order

1. _____ 6. _____

2. _____ 7. _____

3. _____ 8. _____

4. _____ 9. _____

5. _____ 10. _____

...Appointments • Schedule • Notes...

JOB HISTORY OUTLINE

This worksheet will provide the information you will need for your resume. Take your time here as this is your central focus. It is only by examining your experiences in depth, that you can get to the core of your accomplishments, and present them in a way that shows how strong your qualifications are. As you work, be aware of the need for accuracy. There is nothing that will destroy your chances more quickly for securing the job you want than being caught providing exaggerated or fabricated information.

Following are examples of the type of information for each heading:

Employer:	ABC Accounting, Inc.
Title:	Senior Accountant
Address:	Denver, Colorado (Normally a street and zip are not necessary)
Major Duties:	Responsible for audits, prepared annual reports. Prepared corporate tax returns.
Special Projects:	Data collection and analysis for market research projects. Project budgeting and cost containment. Maintained market research library.
Evidence of Leadership:	Researched, selected and implemented the transition to a fully computerized system for the corporation.

Evidence of Special   I was frequently consulted by clients in their purchase of Skills microcomputers. I wrote DBASEIII programs to augment packaged software.

Accomplishments: Through implementation of a computerized system the company was able to increase client base by 17% while reducing operating costs by 11%.

Awards/Recognition: Employee of the Month

• Job History Worksheets are provided for your use on the following pages.

JOB HISTORY WORKSHEET

Employer: _____ Dates: _____ to _____

City: _____ State: _____

Job Title: _____

Major Duties: _____

_____

_____

_____

Special Projects: _____

Evidence of Leadership:

_____

_____

_____

_____

_____

_____

Evidence of Special Skills:

_____

_____

_____

_____

Company Accomplishments for Which I Was Responsible:

_____

_____

_____

_____

Awards/Special Recognition:

_____

_____

_____

JOB HISTORY WORKSHEET

Employer:_____ Dates:_____to_____

City: _____ State: _____

Job Title:_____

Major Duties: _____

_____

_____

_____

Special Projects: _____

Evidence of Leadership:

_____

_____

_____

_____

_____

Evidence of Special Skills:

_____

_____

_____

_____

Company Accomplishments for Which I Was Responsible:

_____

_____

_____

_____

Awards/Special Recognition:

_____

_____

_____

JOB HISTORY WORKSHEET

Employer:_____ Dates: ____ to _____

City: _____ State: _____

Job Title:_____

Major Duties: _____

_____

_____

_____

Special Projects: _____

Evidence of Leadership:

_____

_____

_____

_____

_____

Evidence of Special Skills:

_____

_____

_____

_____

Company Accomplishments for Which I Was Responsible:

_____

_____

_____

_____

Awards/Special Recognition:

_____

_____

_____

JOB HISTORY WORKSHEET

Employer:_____ Dates:_____ to _____

City: _____ State: _____

Job Title:_____

Major Duties: _____

_____

_____

_____

Special Projects: _____

Evidence of Leadership:

_____

_____

_____

_____

_____

_____

Evidence of Special Skills:

_____

_____

_____

_____

Company Accomplishments for Which I Was Responsible:

_____

_____

_____

_____

Awards/Special Recognition:

_____

_____

_____

JOB HISTORY WORKSHEET

Employer:_____ Dates:_____to_____

City: _____ State: _____

Job Title:_____

Major Duties: _____

_____

_____

_____

Special Projects: _____

Evidence of Leadership:

_____

_____

_____

_____

_____

Evidence of Special Skills:

_____

_____

_____

_____

Company Accomplishments for Which I Was Responsible:

_____

_____

_____

_____

Awards/Special Recognition:

_____

_____

_____

JOB HISTORY WORKSHEET

Employer: _____ Dates: _____ to _____

City: _____ State: _____

Job Title: _____

Major Duties: _____

_____

_____

_____

Special Projects: _____

Evidence of Leadership:

_____

_____

_____

_____

_____

Evidence of Special Skills:

_____

_____

_____

_____

Company Accomplishments for Which I Was Responsible:

_____

_____

_____

_____

Awards/Special Recognition:

_____

_____

_____

JOB HISTORY WORKSHEET

Employer:_____ Dates:_____to_____

City: _____ State: _____

Job Title:_____

Major Duties: _____

_____

_____

_____

Special Projects: _____

Evidence of Leadership:

_____

_____

_____

_____

_____

_____

Evidence of Special Skills:

_____

_____

_____

_____

Company Accomplishments for Which I Was Responsible:

_____

_____

_____

_____

Awards/Special Recognition:

_____

_____

_____

JOB HISTORY WORKSHEET

Employer: _____ Dates: _____ to _____

City: _____ State: _____

Job Title: _____

Major Duties: _____

_____

_____

_____

Special Projects: _____

Evidence of Leadership:

_____

_____

_____

_____

_____

Evidence of Special Skills:

_____

_____

_____

_____

Company Accomplishments for Which I Was Responsible:

_____

_____

_____

_____

Awards/Special Recognition:

_____

_____

_____

JOB HISTORY WORKSHEET

Employer:_____ Dates:_____to_____

City: _____ State: _____

Job Title:_____

Major Duties: _____

_____

_____

_____

Special Projects: _____

Evidence of Leadership:

_____

_____

_____

_____

_____

Evidence of Special Skills:

_____

_____

_____

_____

Company Accomplishments for Which I Was Responsible:

_____

_____

_____

_____

Awards/Special Recognition:

_____

_____

_____

JOB HISTORY WORKSHEET

Employer: _____ Dates: _____ to _____

City: _____ State: _____

Job Title: _____

Major Duties: _____

_____

_____

_____

Special Projects: _____

Evidence of Leadership:

_____

_____

_____

_____

_____

_____

Evidence of Special Skills:

_____

_____

_____

_____

_____

Company Accomplishments for Which I Was Responsible:

_____

_____

_____

_____

Awards/Special Recognition:

_____

_____

_____

BASIC SKILLS CHECK LIST

Here is a cross-section of basic skills. Please read through this suggested list and circle items in which you feel you have competence. Add any other basic skills not listed. *These should be skills you would be willing to use in you work.* As an example, I put myself through college painting...but I avoid it like a plague today.

Reading	Managing others	Caring for children
Writing	Remembering	Caring for aged/sick
Organizing	Classifying	Walking/running
Communicating	Innovating	Growing things
Visualizing	Decorating	Counseling
Convincing others	Working with hands	Using tools
Working with numbers	Meeting deadlines	Drawing
Imagining	Supervising	Entertaining
Driving	Living/working outdoors	Research
Supporting others	Keeping records	Repairing
Cooking	Working with animals	Painting
Following instructions	Helping others	Physical dexterity
Fast learner	Conceptualizing	Analyzing
Traveling	Planning	Singing
Meeting strangers	Acknowledging others	Building
Lifting heavy weights	Problem solving	Dancing
Acting	Understanding new things	Teaching

Use this space to add other skills you have or plan to gain that are not included above i.e. computer hardware, software, typing speed, 10 key, etc.

ACTION VERBS

Action Verbs give your resume and cover letter life. The following list is provided to help you describe your duties, responsibilities and accomplishments. You might wish to circle or highlight those that are most applicable as you prepare your *Job History Worksheets.*

Created	Purchased	Rendered	Obtained	Increased
Instructed	Oversaw	Instructed	Studied	Expanded
Reduced	Installed	Counseled	Improved	Trained
Negotiated	Routed	Received	Consolidated	Devised
Planned	Built	Ordered	Supplied	Corresponded
Sold	Audited	Detected	Invented	Prepared
Completed	Coordinated	Selected	Diagnosed	Maintained
Designed	Researched	Logged	Examined	Interpreted
Consulted	Implemented	Edited	Lectured	Administered
Evaluated	Presented	Distributed	Processed	Interviewed
Calculated	Instituted	Arranged	Reviewed	Advised
Identified	Directed	Disproved	Translated	Discovered
Performed	Managed	Developed	Prescribed	Restored
Constructed	Eliminated	Charted	Conserved	Recommended
Controlled	Provided	Wrote	Represented	Delivered
Dispensed	Solved	Analyzed	Promoted	Arbitrated
Formulated	Determined	Produced	Recorded	Criticized
Improved	Collected	Conducted	Operated	Assembled
Tested	Referred	Delivered	Supervised	Realized
Protected	Served	Founded	Drew up	Navigated
Obtained	Compounded	Assisted	Organized	Reviewed

If there are other action words that clearly apply to you, and are not on this list, please add them below.

```
                                                                  
                                                                  
                                                                  
```

PERSONALITY PROFILE

Review this list of personal attributes with yourself in mind. Not just the *"you"* all of us know, but also the one that *you alone know.* Circle each term that describes an attribute clearly representing a facet of your persona.

Willing	Perceptive
Able	Imaginative
Thorough	Creative
Precise	Fast
Careful	Diligent
Energetic	Intelligent
Honest	Determined
Hardworking	Intuitive
Dedicated	Forthright
Insightful	Tenacious
Assertive	Responsible
Sensitive	Incisive
Supportive	Persistent
Able to produce results	Warm
Trustworthy	Friendly
Intent	Humorous
Masterful	Intellectual
Communicative	Analytical
Helpful	Persuasive
Easygoing	Organized
Strong	Flexible

Add any other attributes not listed above that apply to you and list them below:

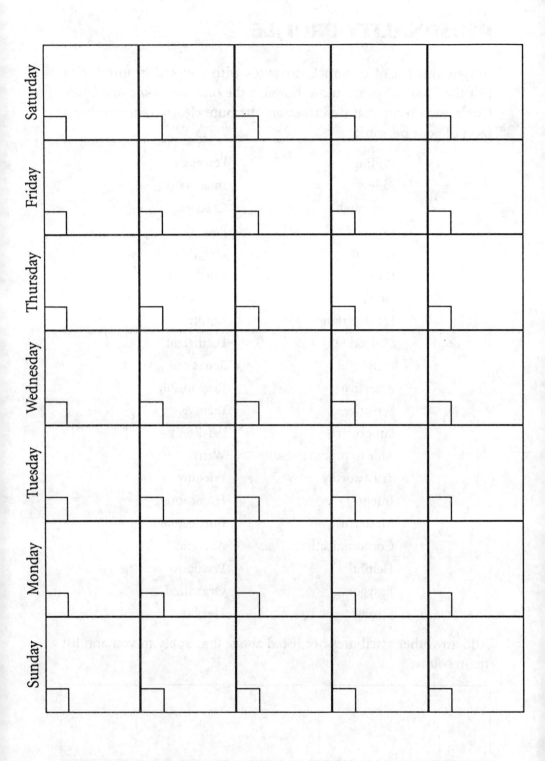

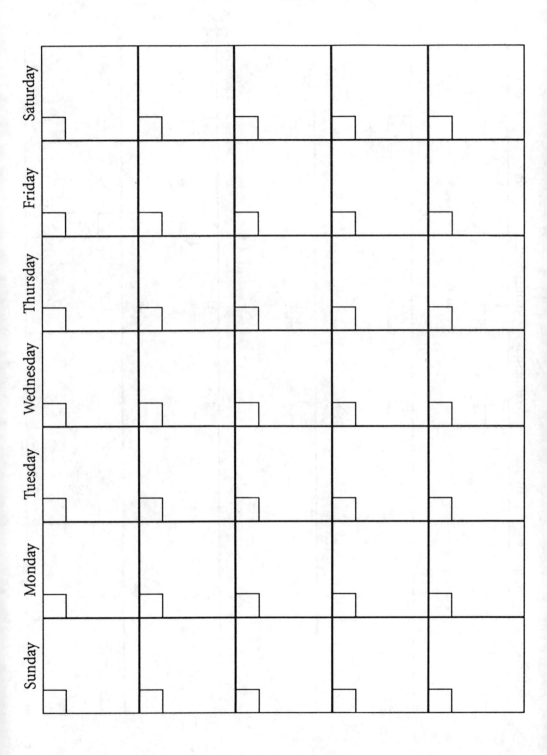

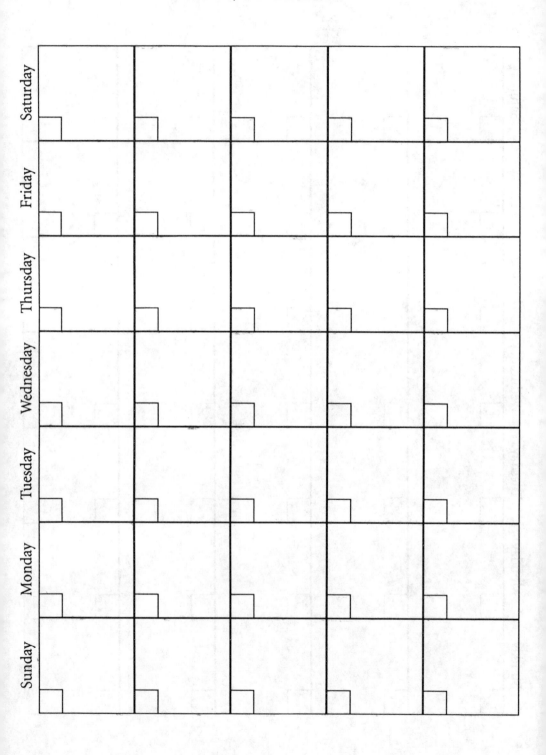

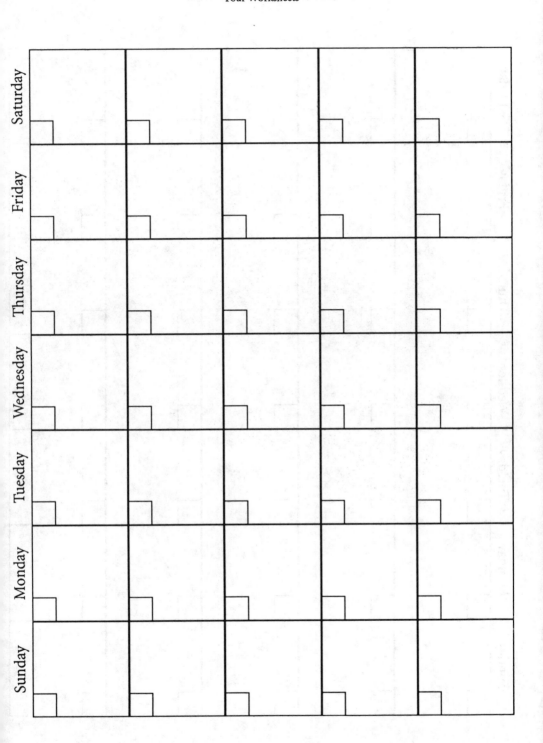

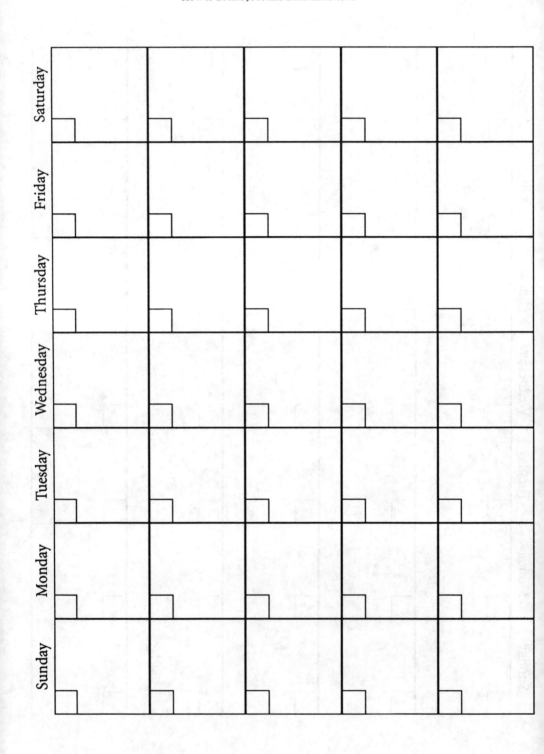

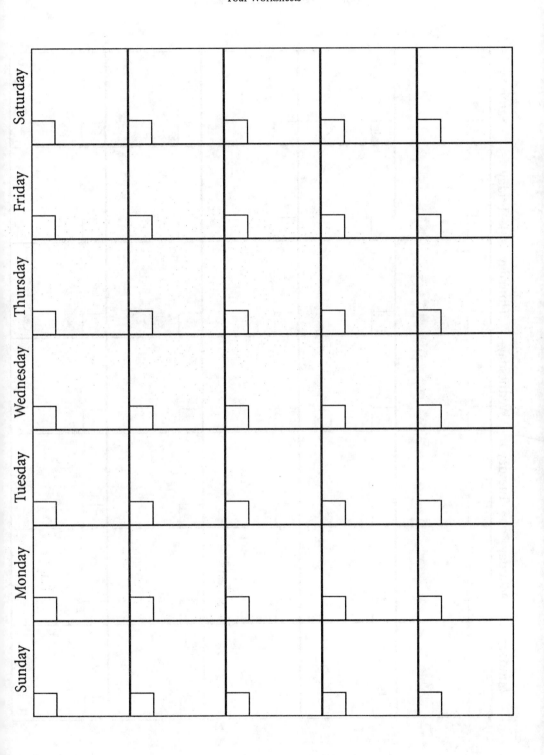

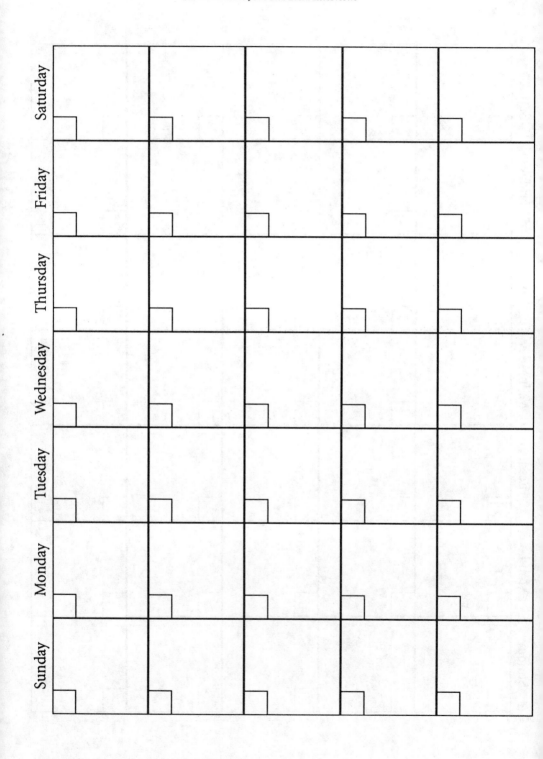

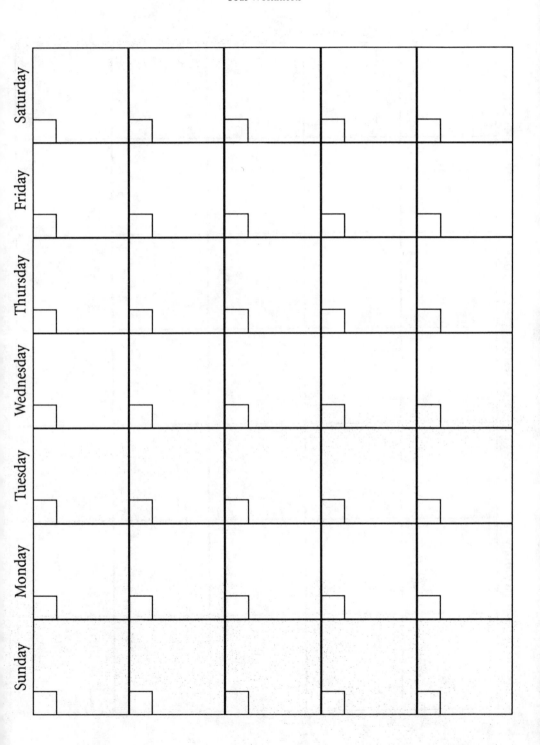

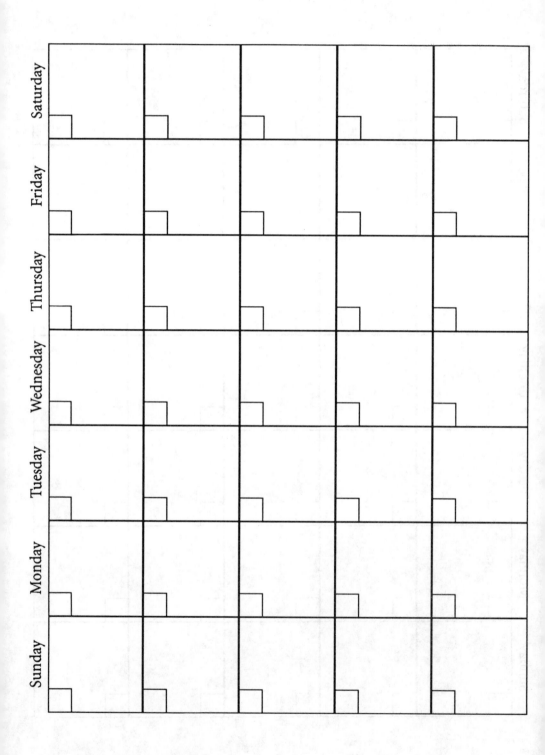

...Sources and Resources...

Your Key to Unlocking the "Hidden Job Market"

- State "Business-to-Business" Directories and
- State Government Employment Offices
- Additional Job Assistance Resources for
    - Career Planning
    - Job Leads
    - Special Networking, Support and Training
      Including:
        ...The Displaced Homemaker...
        ...The Senior/Older Worker...
        ...The Disabled Worker...
        ...Databanks...

1. STATE AND LOCAL "BUSINESS TO BUSINESS" DIRECTORIES

On the following pages I have provided a listing of "Business-to-Business" directories available in each state. This listing allows you to locate virtually every business in your own particular locale.

And don't overlook the yellow pages and business lisings in your own telephone directory.

Although the organization of each directory may differ, you will find the basic information necessary for your "direct-contact" job search campaign.

Your librarian will be happy to assist you in locating and using the information you are seeking.

2. GOVERNMENT EMPLOYMENT OFFICES

Job-search assistance, networking and training programs

I have provided the telephone numbers of your state government employment offices and suggest you give them a call. They will provide information and assistance on the wide variety of state services and special programs available in your particular locale.

3. OTHER COMMUNITY RESOURCES

With a little research, you will find a number of community organizations and resources available to you. Your telephone directory can be a very valuable resource tool. Check your local telephone yellow pages index under *Organizations.* My directory lists more than 20 heading , i.e. *Associations, Business & Trade Organizations,*

Church Organizations, Professional, Fraternal, Handicapped, Labor, Women's Organizations, etc. with hundreds of individual listings.

Many community college career centers and United Way agencies offer outreach programs available in even the smallest communities. Like the state employment offices and the organizations mentioned above, they are excellent networking resources. *Ask Questions! Ask Questions! Ask Questions!*

- United Way

    Since United Way's numerous services and programs vary from community to community, you will need to contact your local office for employment, training, networking and support assistance.

- Community Colleges

    Most community colleges provide a rich source for training, support, networking and career counseling. They offer a variety of programs, many free of charge, including job placement services.

ALABAMA

Directories

- **Alabama Mining and Manufacturing Directory**
  Lists thousands of Alabama companies
- **Alabama Business Directory**
  Lists 135,000 businesses in Alabama
- **Guide to Birmingham**
  Published by Birmingham Chamber of Commerce
- **Major Employers Directory: Metropolitan Birmingham**
  Published by Birmingham Chamber of Commerce

State Employment Offices

- Alabama Development Office
  205-263-0048
- Alabama Occupational Information Coordinating Committee
  205-261-2990
- Department of Industrial Relations
  205-261-2990

ALASKA

Directories

- **Alaska Business Directory**
  Lists 26,000 businesses in Alaska

ARIZONA

Directories

- **Arizona Business Directory**
  Lists 127,000 businesses in Arizona
- **Arizona Directory of Exporters**
  Lists thousands of Arizona based manufacturers

- **Arizona Industrial Directory**
  Lists Arizona manufacturers and wholesalers
- **MacRAE'S State Directories - Arizona, New Mexico**
  Lists over 2,100 firms and 5,000 executives in Arizona and New Mexico
- **Lead Source Inc., City Directories Phoenix, Tucson**
  Phoenix: Lists 40,207 firms and 60,310 executives
  Tucson: Lists 16,328 firms and 24,492 executives

State Employment Offices

- Arizona State Occupational Information Coordinating Committee
  Note: publishes *Associations: Another Job Source,* which lists 140 associations providing career and employment information.
  602-255-3616
- Labor Market Information Research and Analysis Section
  602-255-3616

ARKANSAS

Directories

- **Arkansas Business Directory**
  List 83,000 businesses in Arkansas
- **Directory of Arkansas Manufacturers**
  Lists thousands of manufacturers.
- **MacRAE'S State Directories - Arkansas**
  Lists over 1,700 firms and 5,000 executives in Arkansas

State Employment Offices

- Arkansas Department of Labor
  501-371-1541

- Arkansas Occupational Information Coordinating Committee
501-371-3551

CALIFORNIA

Directories

- **Bay Area Employer Directory**
Lists top Bay Area employers
- **California Manufacturers Register**
Lists thousands of California manufacturers
- **Contacts Influential**
North Orange County: Lists 29,626 firms
Certral Orange County: Lists 30,818 firms
South Orange County: Lists 33,525 firms
Riverside area: Lists 10,089 firms and 15,133 executives
North San Diego: Lists 22,050 firms
South San Diego: Lists 53,186 firms
- **Directory of Major Employers**
- **Directory of Major Manufacturers**
- **Directory of Selected Businesses in Contra Costa County**
- **Hispanic Yellow Pages**
Free directory – 415-626-4111
- **Industrial Directory for Stockton and San Joaquin County**
- **Orange County Business and Industrial Directory**
- **Orange County Media Directory**
- **Red Book of Orange County Business**
- **San Diego Chamber of Commerce, Business Referral Directory**
- **San Diego Creative Directory**
- **San Fernando Valley Industry Guide**
- **San Francisco Industry and Commerce Directory**
- **San Mateo County Commerce and Industry**
- **Santa Clara County Commerce and Industry Directory**
- **Sonoma County Economic Development Board - Directory of Manufacturers**

- **Southern California Business Directory and Buyers Guide**
- **Trade and Professional Associations in California: A Directory**
  Lists state and local trade and professional associations and California offices of national associations
- **The Union-Tribune's Annual Review of San Diego Business**
  Annual round-up of San Diego business, including company names and addresses

State Employment Offices

- California Occupational Information Coordinating Committee
  916-323-6544
- Employment Data and Research Division
  Employment Development Department
  916-427-4675

COLORADO

Directories

- **Colorado Business Directory**
  Lists 154,000 businesses in Colorado
- **Colorado Construction Directory**
- **Contacts Influential**
  Denver Metro: Lists 58,000 firms and 42,000 executives in Denver Metro
  Front Range: Boulder, Colorado Springs, Fort Collins: Lists 30,000 firms
- **Directory of Colorado manufacturers**
  Lists thousands of Colorado manufacturers
- **MacRAE'S State Directories , Colorado, Utah, Nevada**
  Lists over 5,600 firms and 6,600 executives in Colorado, Utah, and Nevada
- **Lead Source Inc., City Directories**

State Employment Offices

- Colorado Division of Employment and Training
    303-866-6316 Contact Chief
- Colorado Occupational Information Coordinating Committee
    303-866-4488 Contact Director

CONNECTICUT

Directories

- **Connecticut Business Directory**
    Lists 135,000 businesses in Connecticut
- **Connecticut Manufacturing Directory, Connecticut Labor Department**
    Lists thousands of manufacturers
- **Connecticut Rhode Island Directory of Manufacturers**
- **Connecticut Service Directory**
    Lists thousands of leading Connecticut service companies
- **Directory of Connecticut Manufacturers**
    Lists top Connecticut manufacturers
- **MacRAE'S State Directories - Connecticut**
    Lists over 4,900 firms and 16,000 executives in Connecticut

State Employment Offices

- Connecticut Department of Labor
    203-566-2120 Contact: Director of Research and Information
- Connecticut Occupational Information Coordinating Committee
    203-638-4042 Contact: Executive Director

DELAWARE

Directories

- **Delaware Business Directory**
    Lists 22,000 businesses in Delaware

- **Delaware Directory of Commerce & Industry**
  Lists leading Delaware companies
- **McRAE'S State Directories, Maryland/D.C./Delaware**
  Lists over 3,100 firms and 8,400 executives in Maryland, Washington, D.C. and Delaware

State Employment Offices

- Delaware Department of Labor
  302-368-6962 Contact: Chief

FLORIDA

Directories

- **Florida Business Directory**
  Lists 528,000 businesses in Florida
- **Contacts Influential**
  Orlando area: Lists 50,835 firms
  Hillsborough: Lists 30,209 firms
  Pinellas: Lists 29,555 firms
- **Directory of Florida Industries**
  Lists thousands of Florida industrial companies
- **Directory of Industries, Tampa and Greater Tampa Metropolitan Area**
- **Directory of Manufacturing and Related Industries**
- **Florida Business Guide and Florida Industries Guide**
  Lists thousands of Florida companies
- **Florida Manufacturers Register**
  Lists 13,000 Florida manufacturers

State Employment Offices

- Bureau of Research and Information
  904-488-4398 Contact: Chief

- Florida Occupational Information System
   904-487-2730 Contact: Director

GEORGIA

Directories

- **Georgia Business Directory**
   Lists 210,000 businesses in Georgia
- **Atlanta Employment Services**
   Lists 70 executive search firms, employment agencies, etc.
- **Georgia Manufacturing Directory**
   Lists 5,000 Georgia manufacturers
- **Greater Atlanta's Best**
- **Major Atlanta Headquartered Firms**
- **Savannah Area Manufacturers Directory**
- **Southern Banker's Directory**

State Employment Offices

- Georgia Department of Labor
   404-656-3177 Contact: Director
- Georgia Occupational Information Coordinating Committee
   404-656-3177

HAWAII

Directories

- **Hawaii Business Directory**
   Lists 44,000 businesses in Hawaii
- **Directory of Manufacturers**
   Lists thousands of Hawaii manufacturers
- **Hawaii Advertising Agency Directory**
- **Hawaii Business Directory**
   Lists 40,000 corporations

State Employment Offices

- Department of Labor and Industrial Relations
  808-548-7639 Contact: Chief
- Hawaii State Occupational Information Coordinating Committee
  808-548-3496 Contact: Executive Director

IDAHO

Directories

- **Idaho Business Directory**
  Lists 43,000 businesses in Idaho
- **Directory of Idaho Manufacturers**
  Lists Idaho manufacturers
- **MacRAE'S State Directories , Idaho, Montana, Wyoming**
  Lists over 2,100 firms and 2,800 executives in Idaho, Montana, and Wyoming

State Employment Offices

- Idaho Department of Employment
  208-544-2755 Contact: Chief
- Idaho Occupational Information Coordinating Committee
  208-334-3705 Contact: Director

ILLINOIS

Directories

- **Downstate Business Directory and Chicago Area Business Directory**
  Lists 373,000 businesses in Illinois: 148,000 Downstate; 243,000 Chicago Area
- **Chicago Banks Directory**
- **Chicago Creative Directory**

- **Chicago, Cook County & Illinois Industrial Directory**
- **Chicago Geographic Edition of the Illinois Manufacturers Directory**
  Lists thousands of Chicago-area manufacturers
- **Greater O'Hare Association of Industry and Commerce Business Directory**
- **How to Get a Job in Chicago**
  Lists major Chicago employers, employment agencies, network groups, and associations
- **Lead Source Inc., City Directories**
  Chicago: Lists 37,468 firms and 56,202 executives
  Suburban North: Lists 39,087 firms and 58,630 executives
  Subruban W/S: Lists 39,915 firms and 59,872 executives
  Outlining areas: Lists 32,356 firms and 48,534 executives
- **Illinois Manufacturers Directory**
  20,000+ listings of Illinois manufacturers
- **Illinois Services Directory**
  Lists thousands of Illinois service companies.
- **MacRAE'S State Directories - Illinois**
  Lists over 9,500 firms and 12,200 executives in Illinois
- **Major Employers in Metropolitan Chicago**

State Employment Offices

- llinois Bureau of Employment Security - Research and Analysis Division
  312-793-2316 Contact: Director
- Illinois Occupational Information Coordinating Committee
  217-785-0789 Contact: Executive Director

INDIANA

Directories

- **Indiana Business Directory**
  Lists 191,000 businesses in Indiana
- **Indiana Industrial Directory**
  Lists thousands of Indiana industrial companies
- **Indiana Manufacturers Directory**
  Lists thousands of Indiana manufacturers
- **MacRAE'S State Directories, Indiana**
  Lists over 9,500 firms and 15,200 executives in Indiana

Indiana Government Employment Offices

- Indiana Employment Security Division - Labor Market Information and Statistical Services, 317-232-7701 Contact: Chief
- Indiana Occupational Information Coordinating Committee 317-232-0173 Contact: Executive Director

IOWA

Directories

- **Iowa Business Directory**
  Lists 118,000 businesses in Iowa
- **Directory of Iowa Manufacturers Iowa Department of Economic Development**
  Lists thousands of Iowa manufacturers
- **Iowa Manufacturers Register**
- **MacRAE'S State Directories, Iowa, Nebraska**
  Lists over 5,000 firms and 5,800 executives in Iowa and Nebraska

State Employment Offices

- Iowa Department of Job Services Research and Statistics
  515-281-8181 Contact: Manager
- Iowa Occupational Information Coordinating Committee
  515-281-8076 Contact: Executive Director

KANSAS

Directories

- **Kansas Business Directory**
  Lists 107,000 businesses in Kansas
- **Directory of Kansas Manufacturers and Products**
  Lists thousands of Kansas manufacturers
- **Fortune 500 Facilities in Kansas**
  Free publication listing Fortune 500 companies in Kansas
- **MacRAE'S State Directories, Kansas**
  Lists over 3,300 firms and 6,800 executives in Kansas
- **Wichita Area Directory of Manufacturers**
- **Wichita Business Journal - Book of Top 25 Lists**
  Yearly publication that lists area businesses ranked in their fields

State Employment Offices

- Kansas Department of Human Resources
  913-296-5061 Contact: Chief, Research and Analysis
- Kansas Occupational Information Coordinating Committee
  913-296-3428 Contact: Director

KENTUCKY

Directories

- **Kentucky Business Directory**
  Lists 109,000 businesses in Kentucky

- **Kentucky Chamber of Commerce Directory**
  Includes information on state business associations
- **Kentucky Directory of Manufacturers**
  Lists thousands of Kentucky manufacturers
- **Kentucky Manufacturers Register**
  List 4,000 Kentucky manufacturers

State Employment Offices

- Department for Employment Services, Labor Market
  Research and Analysis Branch, 502-564-7976 Contact:
  Manager
- Kentucky Occupational Information Coordinating Committee
  502-564-4258 Contact: Coordinator

LOUISIANA

Directories

- **Louisiana Business Directory**
  Lists 142,000 businesses in Louisiana
- **Directory of Louisiana Manufacturers**
  Lists thousands of Louisiana manufacturers
- **New Orleans City Business Reference Guide**
  Lists top area public and private companies

Louisiana Government Employment Offices

- Louisiana State Department of Labor, Research and Statistics
  Section
  504-342-3140 Contact: Director
- Louisiana Occupational Information Coordinating Committee
  504-342-5151 Contact: Coordinator

MAINE

Directories

- **Maine Business Directory**
  Lists 51,000 businesses in Maine
- **Maine Manufacturing Directory**
- **Maine Marketing Directory**
- **Maine, Vermont, New Hampshire Directory of Manufacturers**
  Lists thousands of manufacturers based in the tri-state region
- **McRAE'S State Directories, Maine/New Hampshire/Vermont**
  Lists 2,300 firms and 7,100 executives in Maine, New Hampshire and Vermont

State Employment Offices

- Maine Department of Labor - Division of Research and Analysis, Bureau of Employment Security, 207-289-2271
  Contact: Director
- Maine Occupational Information Coordinating Committee 207-289-2331 Contact: Executive Director

MARYLAND

Directories

- **Maryland Business Directory**
  Lists 151,000 businesses in Maryland
- **Contacts Influential, City Directories, Baltimore/Annapolis/Townson**
  Lists 72,216 firms
- **Directory of Maryland Manufacturers**
- **Lead Source, Inc., City Directories, D.C., Maryland, Baltimore**
  Baltimore: Lists 41,161 firms and 61,741 executives
  Metro D.C.: Lists 36,448 firms and 54,672 executives
  Northern Va: Lists 22,163 firms and 33,244 executives

- **MacRAE'S State Directories, Maryland/D.C./Delaware**
  Lists over 3,100 firms and 8,400 executives in Maryland, Washington, D.C. and Delaware

State Employment Offices

- Maryland Department of Human Resources - Research and Analysis Division
  301-383-5000 Contact: Director
- Maryland Occupational Information Coordinating Committee
  301-383-6730 Contact: Executive Director

MASSACHUSETTS

Directories

- **Massachusetts Business Directory**
  Lists 213,000 businesses in Massachusetts
- **Bank Directory of New England**
- **Boston Job Bank**
  Lists hundreds of Boston-area companies
- **Directory of New England Manufacturers**
  Lists thousands of New England-based manufacturers
- **Directory of Massachusetts Manufacturers**
  Lists thousands of Massachusetts manufacturers
- **Greater Boston Chamber of Commerce-Membership Directory and Buyers Guide**
- **High Technology Careers in Massachusetts**
  Covers high-tech industries in Massachusetts
- **Lead Source, Inc., City Directories**
  Boston North: Lists 45,845 firms and 68,131 executives
  Boston South: Lists 43,845 firms and 65,767 executives
- **McRAE'S State Directories Massachusetts/Rhode Island**
  Lists over 8,600 firms and 25,100 executives in Massachusetts and Rhode Island

- **Major Employers in Greater Boston**
  Lists hundreds of local companies
- **Massachusetts Service Directory**
  Lists thousands of service companies in Massachusetts
- **Massachusetts Manufacturing Directory**
  Lists thousands of Massachusetts manufacturers
- **New England Business, The President's Report**
  Lists New England's top firms
- **The Job Guide**
  Three-volume career guide

State Employment Offices

- Massachusetts Division of Employment Security-Job Market Research and Policy
  617-727-6556 Contact: Director
- Massachusetts Occupational Information Coordinating Committee
  617-727-6718 Contact: Director

MICHIGAN

Directories

- **Michigan Business Directory**
  Lists 307,000 businesses in Michigan
- **Directory of Michigan Manufacturers**
  Lists manufacturers based in Michigan
- **Harris Michigan Industrial Directory**
  Lists thousands of Michigan companies
- **Lead Source, Inc., City Directories**
  Detroit North: Lists 24,935 firms and 37,402 executives
  Detroit South: Lists 19,967 firms and 29,950 executives

- **MacRAE'S State Directories, Michigan**
  Lists over 11,900 firms and 22,500 executives in Michigan
- **Michigan Petroleum Directory**

State Employment Offices

- Michigan Employment Security Commission - Research and
  Statistics Division
  313-876-5445 Contact: Director
- Michigan Occupational Information Coordinating Committee
  517-373-0363 Contact: Executive Coordinator

MINNESOTA

Directories

- **Minnesota Business Directory**
  Lists 162,000 businesses, 5,000 manufacturers plus
  owner/manager contact names
- **Contacts Influential , Minneapolis/St. Paul**
  Minneapolis: Lists 42,123 firms
  St. Paul: Lists 23,657 firms
- **Corporate Report Fact Book**
  Yearly guide to Minnesota business
- **MacRAE'S State Directories, Minnesota**
  Lists over 4,800 firms and 10,600 executives in Minnesota
- **Minnesota Manufacturers Directory**
  Lists thousands of Minnesota manufacturers

State Employment Offices

- Minnesota Department of Jobs and Training, Research and
  Statistical Services Office
  612-296-6545 Contact: Director
- Minnesota Occupational Information Coordinating Committee
  612-296-2072 Contact: Director

MISSISSIPPI

Directories

• **Mississippi Business Directory**
　　Lists 79,000 businesses in Mississippi

• **Mississippi Manufacturers Directory**
　　Lists thousands of Mississippi manufacturers.

State Employment Offices

• Mississippi Division of Employment Security, Labor Market Information Department
　　601-961-7424 Contact: Chief

• Mississippi Occupational Information Coordinating Committee
　　601-359-3412 Contact: Executive Director

MISSOURI

Directories

• **Missouri Business Directory**
　　Lists 202,000 businesses in Missouri

• **Contacts Influential , Kansas City**
　　Kansas City: Lists 47,549 firms

• **Large Employers of Metro St. Louis**
• **Missouri Manufacturers Directory**
　　Lists thousands of Missouri manufacturers

• **Sorkin's Directory of Business and Government, Kansas City Edition**
• **MacRAE'S State Industrial Directory, Missouri**
　　Lists 5,000 firms, 7,500 executives

State Employment Offices

- Missouri Division of Employment Security - Research and Analysis
  314-751-3591 Contact: Chief
- Missouri Occupational Information Coordinating Committee
  314-751-3800 Contact: Director

MONTANA

Directories

- **Montana Business Directory**
  Lists 37,000 businesses in Montana
- **MacRAE'S State Directories, Idaho/Montana/Wyoming**
  Lists over 2,100 firms and 2,800 executives in Idaho, Montana and Wyoming
- **Montana Directory of Manufacturers**
  Lists Montana manufacturers

State Employment Offices

- Department of Labor and Industry, Research and Analysis
  406-444-2661 Contact: Chief
- Montana Occupational Information Coordinating Committee
  406-444-2741 Contact: Program Manager

NEBRASKA

Directories

- **Nebraska Business Directory**
  Lists 68,000 businesses in Nebraska
- **Directory of Manufacturers, Omaha, Nebraska**

- **MacRAE'S State Directories, Iowa/Nebraska**
  Lists over 5,000 firms and 5,800 executives in Iowa and
  Nebraska
- **Nebraska Directory of Manufacturers and their Products**
  Lists Nebraska based manufacturers

State Employment Offices

- Nebraska Department of Labor, Research and Statistics
  402-475-8451 Contact: Chief
- Nebraska Occupational Information Coordinating Committee
  402-475-8451 Contact: Administrator

NEVADA

Directories

- **Nevada Business Directory**
  Lists 41,000 businesses in Nevada
- **MacRAE'S State Directories, Colorado/Utah/Nevada**
  Lists over 5,600 firms and 6,600 executives in Colo., Utah,
  and Nevada
- **Nevada Industrial Directory**
  Lists leading Nevada industrial companies

State Employment Offices

- Nevada Employment Security Department, Employment
  Security Research
  702-885-4550 Contact: Chief
- Nevada Occupational Information Coordinating Committee
  702-885-4577 Contact: Director

NEW HAMPSHIRE

Directories

- **MacRAE'S State Directories, Maine/New Hampshire/Vermont**
  Lists over 2,300 firms and 7,100 executives in Maine, New Hampshire and Vermont

- **Maine, Vermont, New Hampshire Directory of Manufacturers**
  Lists manufacturers in the tri-state area

- **New Hampshire Business Directory**
  Lists 49,000 businesses in New Hampshire

- **New Hampshire Directory of Manufacturers**
  Lists thousands of New Hampshire-based manufacturers

State Employment Offices

- New Hampshire Department of Employment Security, Economic Analysis and Reports
  603-224-3311 Contact: Director

- New Hampshire Occupational Information Coordinating Committee
  603-228-9500 Contact: Director

NEW JERSEY

Directories

- **New Jersey Business Directory**
  Lists 298,000 businesses in New Jersey

- **Directory of New Jersey Manufacturers**
  Lists thousands of manufacturers

- **McRAE'S State Directories, New Jersey**
  Lists over 10,000 firms and 34,000 executives in New Jersey

- **New Jersey Directory of Manufacturers**
  Lists thousands of New Jersey manufacturers

State Employment Offices

- New Jersey Department of Labor-Division of Planning and Research
    609-272-2643 Contact: Director
- New Jersey Occupational Information Coordinating Committee
    609-292-2682 Contact: Staff Director

NEW MEXICO

Directories

- **New Mexico Business Directory**
    Lists 55,000 businesses in New Mexico
- **MacRAE'S State Directories, Arizona/New Mexico**
    Lists over 2,100 firms and 5,000 executives in Arizona and New Mexico
- **New Mexico Directory of Manufacturing and Mining**
    Lists manufacturing and mining companies based in New Mexico
- **New Mexico Manufacturing Directory**
    Lists thousands of New Mexico manufacturers
- **The New Mexico Job Hunter's Guide**
    Includes the state's economic outlook, employment out-looks, information on training and education, and New Mexico-based major employers

State Employment Offices

- Employment Security Department, Economic Research and Analysis
    505-841-8647 Contact: Chief
- New Mexico Occupational Information Coordinating Committee
    505-841-8388 Contact: Executive Director

NEW YORK

Directories

- **Dalton's New York Metropolitan Directory**
  Lists thousands of New York and northern New Jersey companies

- **Greater New York Regional Industrial Buying Guide**
  Lists industrial suppliers, manufacturers, service companies, distributors

- **Long Island Association Membership Directory and Buyers Guide**
  Lists Long Island-based companies

- **The New York State Directory**
  Lists thousands of New York companies

- **MacRAE'S State Directories, New York**
  Lists over 14,000 firms and 48,000 executives in New York

- **Metro New York Directory of Manufacturers**
  Lists thousands of metropolitan New York-based manufacturers

- **New York Manufacturers Directory**
  Lists thousands of New York manufacturers

State Employment Offices

- New York State Department of Labor, Division of Research and Statistics
  518-457-6181 Contact: Director

- New York Occupational Information Coordinating Committee
  518-457-6182 Contact: Executive Director

NORTH CAROLINA

Directories

- **North Carolina Business Directory**
    Lists 248,000 businesses in North Carolina
- **Directory of Manufacturing Firms in North Carolina**
    Lists thousands of North Carolina manufacturing companies
- **Getting Started: North Carolina Jobs and Careers**
    Includes job descriptions, salaries, requirements, employ-
    ment outlook
- **MacRAE'S State Directories, North Carolina/South Carolina/
    Virginia**
    Lists over 10,000 firms and 25,000 executives in N. Carolina,
    S. Carolina, and Virginia
- **Who's Who in Business and Industry in Charlotte**

State Employment Offices

- Employment Security Commission of N. Carolina, Labor Market
  Information Division
    919-733-2936 Contact: Director
- North Carolina Occupational Information Coordinating
  Committee
    919-733-6700 Contact: Director

NORTH DAKOTA

Directories

- **North Dakota Business Directory**
    Lists 29,000 businesses in North Dakota
- **Career Outlook**
    Free annual guide to several hundred occupations including
    descriptions, requirements employment outlook, salaries, etc.

- **MacRAE'S State Directories, North Dakota/South Dakota**
    Lists over 1,900 firms and 3,000 executives in North and
    South Dakota

State Employment Offices

- Job Service North Dakota, Research and Statistics
    701-224-2868 Contact: Chief
- North Dakota Occupational Information Coordinating
    Committee
    701-224-2733 Contact: Director

OHIO

Directories

- **Ohio Business Directory**
    Lists 361,000 businesses in Ohio
- **Columbus Area Employment Resource Directory**
- **Dayton Area Chamber of Commerce - Membership Directory
    and Buyer's Guide**
- **Greater Cincinnati Chamber of Commerce Business and
    Industry Directory**
- **Harris Ohio Industrial Directory**
    Lists thousands of Ohio industrial companies

- **Lead Source, Inc., City Directories, Cleveland, Akron, Canton**
    Cleveland East: Lists 24,525 firms and 36,787 executives
    Cleveland West: Lists 19,721 firms and 29,581 executives
    Akron/Canton: Lists 23,898 firms and 35,847 executives

- **Ohio Manufacturers Directory**
    Lists nearly 20,000 Ohio manufacturers, 48,000 executives

- **Toledo Membership Directory and Buyers Guide**

State Employment Offices

- Ohio Bureau of Employment Services, Labor Market Information Division
    614-466-8806 Contact: Director
- Ohio Occupational Information Coordinating Committee
    614-466-8806 Contact: Director

OKLAHOMA

Directories

- **Oklahoma Business Directory**
    Lists 134,000 businesses in Oklahoma
- **MacRAE'S State Directories, Oklahoma**
    Lists over 2,800 firms and 2,200 executives in Oklahoma
- **Oklahoma Directory of Manufacturers and Processors**
    Lists Oklahoma manufacturers; indexed alphabetically, geographically, and by industry

State Employment Offices

- Oklahoma Occupational Information Coordinating Committee
    405-521-3763 Contact: Executive Directory
- Oklahoma Employment Security Commission, Research and Planning Division
    405-521-3735 Contact: Chief

OREGON

Directories

- **Oregon Business Directory**
    Lists 123,000 businesses in Oregon
- **Contacts Influential, Portland, Willimott Valley**
    Portland: Lists 55,230 firms
    Willamette Valley: Lists 23,170 firms

- **Directory of Occupational and Educational Information Sources**
    Lists state occupational and educational information sources
- **Directory of Oregon Manufacturers**
    Lists thousands of Oregon manufacturers
- **Largest Employers of the Portland Metro Area - Portland Chamber of Commerce**
- **MacRAE'S State Directories, Oregon**
    Lists over 4,800 firms and 9,900 executives in Oregon
- **Manufacturer's Directory for the Portland Metro Area**
- **Portland Chamber of Commerce - Membership Directory**

State Employment Offices

- Department of Human Resources, Employment Division
    503-378-3220 Contact: Administrator
- Oregon Occupational Information Coordinating Committee
    503-378-8146 Contact: Executive Director

PENNSYLVANIA

Directories

- **Pennsylvania Business Directory**
    Lists 392,000 businesses in Pennsylvania

- **Harris Pennsylvania Industrial Directory**
    Lists thousands of industrial companies in Pennsylvania

- **MacRAE'S State Directories, Pennsylvania**
    Lists over 10,400 firms and 36,700 executives in Pennsylvania

- **Major Firms in the Pittsburgh Metro Area**
- **Pennsylvania Manufacturers Register**
    18,000 listings, 41,000 executives

- **Philadelphia Business Journal, Book of Business Lists**

State Employment Offices

- Pennsylvania Department of Labor and Industry, Research and Statistics Division
    717-787-3265 Contact: Chief
- Pennsylvania Occupational Information Coordinating Committee
    717-783-8384 Contact: Director

RHODE ISLAND

Directories

- **Rhode Island Business Directory**
    Lists 37,000 businesses in Rhode Island
- **Connecticut, Rhode Island Directory of Manufacturers**
    Lists thousands of manufacturers in Connecticut and Rhode Island
- **MacRAE'S State Directories, Massachusetts/Rhode Island**
    Lists over 8,600 firms and 25,100 executives in Massachusetts and Rhode Island
- **Rhode Island Directory of Manufacturers**
    Lists thousands of Rhode Island manufacturers

State Employment Offices

- Rhode Island Department of Employment Security, Employment Security Research
    401-277-3704 Contact: Supervisor
- Rhode Island Occupational Information Coordinating Committee
    401-272-0830 Contact: Director

SOUTH CAROLINA

Directories

- **South Carolina Business Directory**
    Lists 119,000 businesses in South Carolina
- **MacRAE'S State Directories, North Carolina/South Carolina/ Virginia**
    Lists over 10,000 firms and 25,000 executives in North Carolina, South Carolina and Virginia
- **South Carolina Chamber of Commerce, Directory**
    Lists South Carolina companies that are members of the State Chamber of Commerce
- **Industrial Directory of South Carolina**
    Lists thousands of South Carolina manufacturers

State Employment Offices

- South Carolina Occupational Information Coordinating Committee
    803-758-3165 Contact: Director
- South Carolina Employment Security Commission, Labor Market Information Division
    803-758-8983 Contact: Director

SOUTH DAKOTA

Directories

- **South Dakota Business Directory**
    Lists 31,000 businesses in South Dakota
- **MacRAE'S State Directories, North Dakota/South Dakota**
    Lists over 1,900 firms and 3,000 executives in North and South Dakota
- **South Dakota Directory of Manufacturers and Processors**
    Lists thousands of South Dakota industrial companies

South Dakota Government Employment Offices

- Department of Labor - Labor Market Information Center
  605-622-2314 Contact: Chief
- South Dakota Occupational Information Coordinating
  Committee
  605-622-2314 Contact: Executive Director

TENNESSEE

Directories

- **Tennessee Business Directory**
  Lists 173,000 businesses in Tennessee
- **Directory of Tennessee Manufacturers**
- **Directory of Tennessee Mining and Oil Gas Operations**
- **Directory of Tennessee's Forest Industries**

State Employment Offices

- Tennessee Department of Employment Security, Research and
  Statistics
  615-741-6451 Contact: Chief
- Tennessee Occupational Information Coordinating Committee
  615-741-6451 Contact: Director

TEXAS

Directories

- **Texas Business Directory**
  Lists 683,000 businesses in Texas
- **Dallas County Business Guide**
- **Directory of Manufacturers and Twin Plants**
- **Directory of Texas Manufacturing**
- **Greater Houston Chamber of Commerce, Membership
  Directory and Buyer's Guide**

- **Harris County Business Guide**
- **Houston Business Journal Book of Lists**
  Ranked listings of area businesses, statistics, etc.
- **How to Get a Job in Dallas/Ft. Worth**
  Lists major employers in Dallas/Ft. Worth, employment agencies, network groups, and associations
- **Largest Employers Directory**
- **MacRAE'S State Directories, Texas**
  Lists over 11,900 firms and 16,700 executives in Texas
- **Oil Directory of Texas**
  Lists oil industry companies
- **Tarant County Business Guide**
- **Texas Manufacturers Directory**
  Lists 21,000 plants and 40,000 executives
- **Travis County Business Guide**

State Employment Offices

- Texas Employment Commission, Economic Research and Analysis
  512-397-4540 Contact: Chief
- Texas Occupational Information Coordinating Committee
  512-463-2399 Contact: Director

UTAH

Directories

- **Utah Business Directory**
  Lists 55,000 businesses in Utah
- **MacRAE'S State Directories, Colorado/Utah/Nevada**
  Lists over 5,600 firms and 6,600 executives in Colorado, Utah and Nevada
- **Utah Directory of Business and Industry**
  Lists thousands of Utah companies

State Employment Offices

- Utah Department of Employment Security, Research and Analysis
  801-533-2014 Contact: Chief
- Utah Occupational Information Coordinating Committee
  801-533-2028

VERMONT

Directories

- **Vermont Business Directory**
  Lists 27,000 businesses in Vermont
- **MacRAE'S State Directories, Maine/New Hampshire/Vermont**
  Lists over 2,300 firms and 7,100 executives in Main, New Hampshire and Vermont.
- **Maine, Vermont, New Hampshire Directory of Manufacturers**
  Lists thousands of manufacturers in the tri-state region
- **Vermont Directory of Manufacturers**
  Lists Vermont manufacturers

State Employment Offices

- Vermont Department of Employment and Training, Research and Statistics Section
  802-229-0311 Contact: Chief
- Employment Services Vermont Department of Employment
  802-773-5837
- Vermont Occupational Information Coordinating Committee
  802-229-0311 Contact: Chief

VIRGINIA

Directories

- **Virginia Business Directory**
  Lists 183,000 businesses in Virginia
- **Directory of the Mineral Industry in Virginia**
- **Fairfax County Directory of Business and Industry**
- **Lead Source Inc., City Directories, Northern Virginia**
  Lists 22,163 firms and 33,244 executives
- **MacRAE'S State Directories, North Carolina/ South Carolina/ Virginia**
  Lists over 10,000 firms and 25,000 executives in North Carolina, South Carolina and Virginia
- **Virginia Industrial Directory**
  Lists thousands of Virginia industrial companies

State Employment Offices

- Virginia Employment Commission, Office of Research and Analysis
  804-786-7496 Contact: Director
- Virginia Occupational Information Coordinating Committee
  804-786-3177 Contact: Executive Director

WASHINGTON

Directories

- **Washington Business Directory**
  Lists 179,000 businesses in Washington
- **Contacts Influential**
  Seattle area: Lists 66,940 firms
  Tacoma area: Lists 23,835 firms
- **Directory of Major Employers: Central Puget Sound Region**

- **Directory of Seattle, King County Manufacturers**
  Lists local manufacturers

- **MacRAE'S State Directories, Washington State**
  Lists over 3,800 firms and 7,400 executives in Washington

- **Washington Manufacturers Register**
  Lists thousands of Washington manufacturers

State Employment Offices

- Washington Employment Security Department, Labor Market and Economic Analysis Branch
  206-753-5224 Contact: Director

- Washington Occupational Information Coordinating Committee
  206-754-1552 Contact: Director

WASHINGTON, D.C.

Directories

- **Washington D.C. Business Directory**
  Lists 112,000 businesses in Washington, D.C.

- **Lead Source Inc., City Directories, Metro D.C.**
  Metro DC: Lists 36,448 firms and 54,672 executives

- **Manufacturers Directory, Metropolitan Washington, D.C.**
  Lists leading manufacturers

State Employment Offices

- District of Columbia Occupational Information Coordinating Committee
  202-639-1083 Contact: Executive Director

- Division of Labor Market Information, Research and Analysis
  202-639-1642 Contact: Chief

WEST VIRGINIA

Directories

- **West Virginia Business Directory**
  Lists 52,000 businesses in West Virginia
- **West Virginia Manufacturers Register**
  Lists thousands of West Virginia manufacturers

State Employment Offices

- Labor and Economic Research Section, West Virginia Dept. of Employment Security
  304-348-2660 Contact: Assistant Director
- West Virginia Occupational Information Coordinating Committee
  304-348-0061 Contact: Executive Director

WISCONSIN

Directories

- **Wisconsin Business Directory**
  Lists 188,000 businesses in Wisconsin
- **Classified Directory of Wisconsin Manufacturers**
  Lists thousands of Wisconsin manufacturers
- **MacRAE'S State Directories, Wisconsin**
  Lists over 5,100 firms and 17,200 executives in Wisconsin
- **Metropolitan Milwaukee Association of Commerce, Membership Directory and Buyer's Guide**
  Lists Milwaukee-area companies
- **Racine Area Manufacturers Directory**
- **Wisconsin Manufacturers Directory**
  Nearly 10,000 listings, 24,000 executives

State Employment Offices

- Department of Industry, Labor and Human Relations-Labor Market Information Section
  608-266-5843 Contact: Chief
- Wisconsin Occupational Information Coordinating Committee
  608-266-2439 Contact: Executive Director

WYOMING

Directories

- **Wyoming Business Directory**
  Lists 22,000 businesses in Wyoming
- **MacRAE'S State Directories, Idaho/Montana/Wyoming**
  Lists over 2,100 firms and 2,800 executives in Idaho, Montana and Wyoming
- **Wyoming Directory of Manufacturing and Mining**
  Lists several hundred Wyoming companies

State Employment Offices

- Employment Security Commission, Research and Analysis Section
  307-235-3642 Contact: Chief
- Wyoming Occupational Information Coordinating Committee
  307-777-7574

ADDITIONAL SOURCES OF INFORMATION

In addition to the directories I've listed for each state, there are many specialized business directories available in most business and general libraries. Here is a partial list. Ask your librarian for additional assistance.

- Dun and Bradstreet's Million Dollar Directory
- Standard & Poor's Register of Corporations, Directors and Executives
- Standard Directory of Advertisers
- Thomas Register of American Manufacturers and Thomas Register Catalog File
- U.S. Industrial Directory
- U.S. Manufacturers Directory
- American Register of Exporters and Importers
- Directory of Firms Operating in Foreign Countries
- Dun & Bradstreet's Metalworking Directory
- Battin International: International Business Register
- Dun & Bradstreet's Principal International Businesses
- Fraser's Canadian Trade Directory

- **Occupational Outlook Handbook.** Washington, D.C. This is not a directory of firms or businesses, but is an excellent resource for job descriptions to help in your resume writing or career selection. It includes current information about the numbers of jobs in the fields and sources of information. Related reading are also included.

Here are some books that will help you in your career search and planning. Most can be found in your public library or book store.

What Color is Your Parachute? Bolles, Richard Nelson. The classic guide to job hunting.

How to Get a Job, Make it Big, Do it Now and Love It. Calano, James, and Salzman, Jeff. Excellent guide for new graduates.

Business as a Game. Carr, Albert Z. A classic on getting along with and within big business.

The Rites and Rituals of Corporate Life. Deal, Terrence E., and Kennedy, Allen A. Corporate Cultures: Excellent background reading.

Getting to Yes: Negotiating Agreement Without Giving In. Fisher, Roger, and Ury, William. How you can strike the best possible deal.

101 Great Answers To The Toughest Interview Questions. Fry, Ron. This is a must reference to prepare for your interview.

Guerrilla Tactics in the Job Market. Jackson, Tom. Tactics for playing rough.

How You Really Get Hired. LaFevre, John L. This book shows what matters most to employers and what you must do to get a job offer.

Salary Strategies. Kennedy, Marilyn Moats. An excellent guide from a business consultant.

Jobs '92. Petras, Kathryn & Ross. A brand-new book on career outlooks, industry forecasts and regional roundups for the 1990s.

ADDITIONAL SOURCES FOR JOB LEADS

In addition to the business-to-business directories, here are some additional job lead sources.

- Newspaper classified advertisements
- Business, education, health and other special sections of the newspaper
- Personal contacts through friends and relatives
- Contacts made through projects in school
- Professional and trade journals and newspapers
- Professional association conference placement services (Many provide annual books with listings of resume and job openings)
- College and university placement offices
- Professors and teachers (past and present)
- Private and State employment service agencies
- Federal Job Information Services
- Classified telephone directories (yellow pages)
- Chamber of commerce lists
- Local business journals or newspapers such as, *The Denver Business Journal*
- Unions

Disabled Workers: Alliance for Technology Access
Offers resource centers located in most states. For current information write or call the National Offices:

- 1307 Solano Ave.
  Albany, CA 94706-1888
  (415) 528-0747
  and

- 217 Massachusetts Ave.
  Lexington, MA 02173
  (617) 863-9966

National Networking for the Displaced Homemaker
- Displaced Homemakers Network, National Headquarters
  1010 Vermont Ave. N.W., Suite 817
  Washington, DC 20005

- Catalyst National Headquarters
  14 East 60th St.
  New York, NY 10022

Computer Matching
- *Career System* is a new nationwide computer matching network and data base information system designed to assist employers in identifying qualified professionals to fill jobs. For more information write:

- Career System, Corp.
  Service division
  1675 Palm Beach Lakes Blvd.
  West Palm Beach, FL 33401

Database Mailing Lists
- *American Business Information, Contacts Influential and Jobs On File* Provides detailed, custom data in a variety of formats: mailing lists, computer disks, 3 x 5 cards etc. For information and cost write or call:

- American Business Information
  P.O. Box 27347, Omaha, NE 68127
  (402) 331-7169 FAX (402) 331-1505

- Contacts Influential
  999 18th Street #3280
  Denver, CO 80202-2410
  (303) 297-3927 FAX (303) 291-9629

- Electronic On-Line Business Link
  (402) 593-4593

ADDITIONAL SOURCES
FOR THE OLDER WORKER

The ranks of graying Americans are swelling and this growth will continue well into the 21st century. As a group, our health is better than ever; our minds are alert and creative; we hold a treasure house of experience, talent, energy and skills. Many of us are not ready to step out of the mainstream of life.

Yet many companies today are cutting back or "downsizing" their employment roles. In some cases, the older, experienced worker is facing early retirement. In other cases the experienced worker is just laid off and replaced by a younger, less expensive, employee. Against the law? You bet. *It's called discrimination,* but it happens all the time. This practice can create devastating financial problems.

If you are a senior, be sure to contact AARP local chapters as well as the national headquarters. Check your local telephone directory for local chapters.

Additionally I would like to alert you to the *Senior Community Service Employment* Program, (SCSEP). This is a federally funded program sponsored by 10 national organizations, including AARP. SCSEP is an employment service that pays you for on-the-job training in community service agencies while helping you find a job with private or public employers. SCSEP is active in each county in all 50 states and Puerto Rico. Information, qualifications and application can be secured through your state employment office or by writing:

- AARP/SCSEP,
  1909 K Street N.W.
  Washington, DC, 20049

Another outstanding program is *AARP Works.* The only qualification for this 21-hour workshop is that you be 50 or older. The workshop provides each participant with outstanding instruction, materials and job assistance. Originally, I was a participant and now serve as a volunteer consultant in the Denver area.

For information on availability, dates and locations in your area contact:

- National AARP Works Equity
  1909 K St.. N.W.
  Washington, DC, 20049

In addition be sure to check your phone book for other organizations in your locale. Start with your state employment offices and community colleges. They will provide a wealth of information on senior opportunities in your area.

- State government employment offices
- 40 Plus, a national organization working out of state offices
- Community colleges (Most have outstanding services available for the senior)
- Older Worker Employment Council
- Senior citizen community centers
- Chambers of commerce

Index